BIBLE CHARACTERS AND DOCTRINES

Vashti to Elihu
E. M. BLAIKLOCK, M.A., D.Litt.

The Person of Christ
JAMES PHILIP, M.A.

WILLIAM B. EERDMANS PUBLISHING COMPANY
GRAND RAPIDS, MICHIGAN

© 1973 Scripture Union
First published 1973
First U.S.A. edition June 1973

Library of Congress Catalog Number: 72-189855
ISBN 0-8028-1464-6

SCRIPTURE UNION IN NORTH AMERICA

U. S. A.: 38 Garrett Road, Upper Darby,
           Pennsylvania 19082
Canada: 5 Rowanwood Avenue, Toronto 5,
           Ontario

Printed in the United States of America.

Each volume of Bible Characters and Doctrines is divided into the right number of sections to make daily use possible, though dates are not attached to the sections because of the books' continuing use as a complete set of character studies and doctrinal expositions. The study for each day is clearly numbered and the Bible passage to be read is placed alongside it.

Sections presenting the characters and doctrines alternate throughout each book, providing balance and variety in the selected subjects. At the end of each section there is a selection of questions and themes for further study related to the material covered in the preceding readings.

Each volume will provide material for one quarter's use, with between 91 and 96 sections. Where it is suggested that two sections should be read together in order to fit the three-month period, they are marked with an asterisk.

The scheme will be completed in four years. Professor E. M. Blaiklock, who writes all the character studies, will work progressively through the Old and New Testament records. Writers of the doctrinal sections contribute to a pattern of studies drawn up by the Rev. Geoffrey Grogan, Principal of the Bible Training Institute, Glasgow, in his capacity as Co-ordinating Editor. A chart overleaf indicates how the doctrinal sections are planned.

In this series biblical quotations are normally taken from the RSV unless otherwise identified. Occasionally Professor Blaiklock provides his own translation of the biblical text.

DOCTRINAL STUDY SCHEME

	Year 1	Year 2	Year 3	Year 4
First Quarter	The God who Speaks	Man and Sin	The Work of Christ	The Kingdom and the Church
Second Quarter	God in His World	Law and Grace	Righteousness in Christ	The Mission of the Church
Third Quarter	The Character of God	The Life of Christ	Life in Christ	The Church's Ministry and Ordinances
Fourth Quarter	The Holy Trinity	The Person of Christ	The Holy Spirit	The Last Things

DOCTRINAL STUDIES

THE PERSON OF CHRIST

Study

CHARACTER STUDIES

VASHTI TO ELIHU

Study

CHARACTER STUDIES

1 : Vashti

Esther 1

In Daniel's story of Belshazzar's feast, we met the dignified queen of Babylon, intruding on the scene of debauchery and fear with sane words designed to save her son. Here is the queen of the empire which succeeded Babylon, and a first glimpse of another tyrant on the throne, and new corruption taking Babylon's old path.

If Ahasuerus was Xerxes, we know the madman well. He was the despot who launched the mighty attack on Greece in 480 B.C., and had the Dardanelles branded because its current broke his bridge of boats. This was the invasion which put into European history the brave tale of Thermopylae, with its three hundred Spartans holding the narrow pass, and the battle of Salamis, one of the decisive fights in history, in which Athens and her allies smashed the Persian fleet, and sent the mad king scuttling for home along the death-strewn roads.

His mighty empire lay across the world from the Aegean to the Indus and the Nile. Ahasuerus lived in pomp and glory, fed with flattery by his vicious court, and honoured like a god. This glimpse into that court's evil life shows the corrupted king feasting his base lords, like Belshazzar before him. The eastern world lay in his hands, with vast problems of defence and organization, but here was the most powerful ruler of the day boasting of his wife's beauty, and bidding her make a public display of her person before the revelling men.

Why did Vashti refuse to do so? It was mortally dangerous to defy the order of the brutal king. It seems that she was a noble woman who prized her modesty and self-respect above

9

her royal estate. Moral courage is a rare virtue in this cowardly world, and it requires courage of the first order to set in the balances those qualities of uprightness, integrity and loyalty to the highest against the advantages which men prize—position, status, comfort, wealth and the adulation of the world.

On the other hand, Vashti, entertaining the women in another banqueting hall, may have defied her royal lord in an act of drunken bravado, stimulated by the revelling crowd of women who enjoyed vicariously the taste of female revolt.

But in all history there seems no example of a virtuous court where monarchy is absolute. Power always plays its ancient and corrupting part. Evil cannot be confined, and tyrants corrupt their environment.

2 : Myrtle and Mordecai

Esther 2

Here indeed is a sight for sorrow. The purpose of this vivid book is to show a picture of one section of the Jewish Dispersion. We do not meet them again until the Acts of the Apostles. Nehemiah, Ezra, and Daniel show us another group. Myrtle, the Jewish girl ('Hadassah' [7] has this meaning), was brought up by her shrewd cousin Mordecai. He had provided himself with a pagan name based apparently on that of the god Marduk. It is true that all Jews of the Dispersion took Gentile names; Saul, for example, became Paul, but Jews seldom compromised thus with paganism. Esther's Gentile name appears to exalt the goddess Ishtar. Hence the comment at the beginning of this paragraph. Mordecai succeeded in his ambitions. His cousin was a notable social triumph. Contrary to all Jewish law, she married the heathen king, and Mordecai had his ally in the palace.

Esther is commonly lauded as a heroine of Scripture, and there is no doubting the courage of the Jewish girl, so lamentably married to the megalomaniac who decimated his own empire, and wasted its resources in the mass attack on Europe. A woman so strong was hardly the passive tool of her designing guardian. She should have been able, in the tight community of the Jews, to escape the notice of the king's girl-hunters. The entry of Esther into this disgraceful beauty contest was deliberate. She must have known that union with a pagan was contrary to the code of her people, but here were Jews who sought an accommodation with their environment. Without comment, this vivid book tells the story. Significantly, it avoids all mention of the name of God. The Jews noted this, and Jews of Alexandria, not unlike those who were happy in Susa, invented additions to the story, which include the divine name. The passages may be read in the Septuagint, the Greek version of the Scriptures which the Jews of Alexandria prepared, to astonish their pagan hosts.

The date, contrary to Ussher's guess, could have been 479 B.C. Note 1.3 and 2.16. There is a gap of four years. Could this have been the time during which the Shah was preoccupied with the preparations for his vast assault on Greece, his march, disaster and retreat? It is not unlikely. So it was a badly shaken, as well as a viciously pagan, husband that Esther found, having successfully, on Mordecai's advice, concealed the facts of her nationality (2.10).

3 : Haman

Esther 3

Haman took his cue from his base royal master. He found Mordecai insolent, and in revenge sought to destroy all the people of Mordecai—genocide for offended dignity. Ahasuerus with a wave of the hand gave him permission to commit this immense crime, and to confiscate a people's goods (11). The king, as Herodotus, the Greek historian, described him, was half-insane in his cocoon of absolute sovereignty, and perhaps at the time was mentally exhausted after his retreat from Greece. He was the king of whom Byron wrote:

> *A king sate on the rocky brow*
> *Which looks o'er sea-born Salamis;*
> *And ships, by thousands, lay below,*

And men in nations; all were his!
He counted them at break of day—
And when the sun set, where were they?

The poet referred to the hill west of Athens where the Persian king sat enthroned to watch his fleet in the strait below destroy the Athenians. He saw instead irremediable disaster. His eyes, after that campaign, had ceased to count the toll of dead. What was the massacre of a scattered nation?

But look at the Jew in the royal court. He is a strange sight. There was an element of independence in Mordecai, or perhaps he merely presumed upon his connection with the new queen. His motive for his dangerous act of defiance is difficult to understand on any supposition. It imperilled the Jews unnecessarily, and having gone so far as to seek small service in the palace, and to introduce his ward to the royal harem, it might be supposed that Mordecai had accepted all subservience. But, from whatever motive it was, Mordecai clung to this shred of dignity or obstinacy. He could hardly have calculated the sequence of events which fill the rest of his story.

Haman, at the moment, had the despot's ear, and perhaps he had more motives than resentment against the surly Mordecai. The Jews were obviously rich, and loot was a temptation. This is the first indication in literature of the Jew in that role of moneyman into which Gentile persecution has so often forced an agricultural and pastoral people. Confiscation and pogrom against that shrewd and able people have often resulted, and medieval England was as guilty as ancient Persia in this regard. Haman had many successors.

4 : Mordecai

Esther 4

Mordecai was directly responsible for the grim catastrophe which was about to fall on the Jews of Persia. It is a fact of life that our ill deeds cannot be isolated and contained.

Mordecai should not have been in the exposed position into which his scheming life had led him. He should not have been in confrontation with the vizier Haman. Finding himself in that position, he could at least have conducted himself with discretion. But the whole lamentable situation arose from materialism, the base quest for gain, and activities unworthy of a man of God. His informer's deed (2.21–23) may or may not have done good. Bigthan and Teresh might well have had good reason to strike down the beastly creature who ruled Persia, but to Mordecai they were, for good or ill, two expendable pawns in a game of self-seeking. In the outcome, whether Mordecai did right or wrong in exposing the details of the plot to the king, the service was forgotten, probably during the preoccupations of the war with distant Greece. In the providence of God, whatever Mordecai's immediate motives may have been, the service he rendered became the event God used to save His errant people. The fact that it was thus, in mercy, fitted into a divine overruling, in no way adds sanctity to the life or conduct of Mordecai.

In the face of ugly peril, Mordecai was shrill in his lamentations, and turned to Esther with the nearest expression of a living faith he ever manifested. Esther, he opined, putting a common saying into the world's stock, might have attained to royalty precisely for this purpose. One can imagine with what a rich voice of faith in God, and reverence for His name, Daniel, or Joseph, or Nehemiah, those other Jewish denizens of pagan courts, might have more worthily expressed the same truth. And note with what words Mordecai feels compelled to bracket his appeal. He had no evidence that his ward would be anything other than the brave woman he must have known her to be, but he reminds her that the royal harem is no refuge. Esther made no reproach. She should not have been queen, but, being queen, she acted like a queen. It was not in God's purposes that unbridled wickedness should destroy a remnant of His people, comfortable in a pagan environment though they had become. Esther had courage, and that courage He used.

5 : Esther, the King, and the Vizier

Esther 5 and 6

Under the base despotism of Persia, to enter the royal presence unbidden was contrary to law. In Athens, still moving on joyously in the enthusiasm of the Greek victory over Persia, liberty was taking shape in this century among men. In Ahasuerus' court the evils of tyranny still sat enthroned, and it was peril for the queen herself to enter the audience chamber without a summons. The abominable man upon the dais held his sceptre towards her to signify that her life was spared. Esther was a courageous woman, the forerunner of multitudes who have faced peril in the ghetto for their people. She had also learned some other lessons well. She controlled features and voice, and hid with consummate art her ultimate purpose against Haman. The favourite was quite deceived. He merits little pity, as the sequel shows. His whole spirit was eaten up with his hatred for Mordecai. His wife, too, shared his vices. Hers was the cruel suggestion that now was the hour to glut his vengeance. The Greeks feared a vice which they called *hybris,* that overweening arrogance and self-esteem which go before a fall. Haman was a notable illustration. Pride corrupts the judgement. His mind bent by his own self-esteem, the vizier was in no condition to answer wisely. The twin vices of jealousy and arrogance perverted reason, and with poetic justice brought the wretched man to humiliation. Thought can move in a straight, clean line only when the heart is pure. Vice deflects true judgement from its path, distorts the vision of the goal, and betrays the one who tolerates it. 'You seek honour from one another', said the Lord in a penetrating word, 'therefore you *cannot* believe' (John 5.44). Faith, He meant, is inhibited by pride. The first requirement of those who seek God is self-abandonment and humility. Lacking these, a man lacks all. Pride is a jealous and consuming demon which eats up the whole personality, drags into its orbit of control all activity, all thought, leaving no room for cleaner, nobler, living.

Haman is a pitiable spectacle of human ruin. The king is no better. Awake at night, he feeds his pride on the records of his reign, and so finds out about Mordecai.

6 : Esther Triumphant

Esther 7 and 8

The terrible drama in the vicious court is running inexorably to its conclusion. With consummate self-control Esther held her peace throughout the first day's feasting. Then, on the second day, at the so-called 'banquet of wine', Ahasuerus, like Herod on a similar occasion five centuries later (Mark 6.22 f.), made his customary offer of beneficence.

Esther, who had betrayed no sign of excitement or emotion to this point of time, chose the precise, deadly moment to speak. It is terrible to think what must have been the childhood and youth of a young woman who could have learned such stern self-mastery. Esther was brought up in a school of suffering. Her teachers were the cruel circumstances of a harsh and pitiless pagan environment which had taught her to maintain silence against all provocation, to read the mind of an enemy, to bide her time, and betray her motives and purpose to none, to understand vicious men and use them. Such powers served her and her people well, but a better environment could have been found for the education of a girl in the toil and poverty of far Jerusalem. Haman fell into the snare which he had prepared for others. Judgement sometimes works that way.

Mordecai had won notable success. And yet he is surely a sight for sorrow in the rich livery of the vicious king, 'with a great golden crown' (15) on his head. There are some honours which are not worth winning, and commendation which is base reproach. 'What have I done wrong,' Socrates once remarked, 'that this wicked man should speak well of me?' It is even more sad to see the brave Esther point her appeal with reference to her place in the king's regard—'If I have found favour in your sight, O King . . .' The reversal of the savage royal decree was as irresponsible as its original proclamation had been. Just as the Jews were to be pitilessly massacred, so now were they free to wreak pitiless vengeance on the Persian and other subjects of the tyrant. Human life counted for nothing in his eyes. This is where the sinful human heart ends. All love dies, all mercy. All pity withers in the godless life. All love, all mercy, all pity, wherever they are found, are of God,

When God is banished these qualities fade, as our own times can witness equally with Esther's century.

7 : Esther and Mordecai Triumphant

Esther 9

This is a chapter which any student of the men and women of the Bible would gladly pass over. Esther, in the passion of her revenge, is a hideous spectacle. Haman's ten sons die with their father, and in a second day of massacre the berserk Jews soaked the land in the blood of their enemies. The embittered and the persecuted, who lose touch with God, can fall victim to strange evils of the mind.

If Esther was the Amestris of secular history, the curious can see her similarly at work in another situation of savage revenge. The context is uncannily the same, an offence given, a royal banquet, a mad Herod-like promise to give the gift required, and sadistic vengeance. The hideous tale of how Amestris gained control of her sister-in-law, and horribly mutilated her, causing in the process, the death of the king's brother Masistes, is told boldly in Book 9 of Herodotus, 109–113 (Sir Henry Rawlinson's translation, Everyman's *Herodotus*, pp. 323-325). The human mind is safe only when it lies in the blessed control of the One in whose image it was first made. Shake off that control, and the beast takes over.

But turn the picture round. Forget for a moment the unedifying picture of Esther presiding at a banquet of mass murder, and the contemptible Mordecai, with his dearly bought eminence, faithfully serving one of the most evil men of his day, and see where Haman's mad lust for power had led him. The eighty-three foot high gallows stood as a symbol of judgement upon him. We have noted before, the situation which the Greek, Aristotle, regarded as the very stuff of tragic drama, and which he called *'peripeteia'*. It is sometimes Anglicized into 'peripety', and means that reversal of fortune which comes when those measures men take for their own advantage, or to gain some evil end, produce the exact opposite to their intentions, and recoil upon their own heads. It seems part of the operation of the moral law which God has woven into the processes of life. It is another aspect of the truth of Gal. **6**, that 'whatever a man sows, that he will also reap'. What the end of Esther and Mordecai was we do not know, but may be sure that they, too, were not exempt from God's law—in this world and the next.

Questions and themes for study and discussion on Studies 1–7

1. Vashti and the queen of Babylon. Name three other royal women of Scripture to set with them, and two governors' wives. (Clue: Exodus, Kings, Matthew, Mark, Acts.)
2. The mental and moral damages of power.
3. Revenge. Why does hate destroy the personality? What is the safeguard against it?
4. What is 'worldly wisdom'? Has it any place in Christian service?
5. Is the moral law always visible in life? Is justice always done in this life? What is the significance of the Last Judgement?

THE PERSON OF CHRIST

Introduction

Church history from the earliest times has shown unmistakably that the Person of Christ is central to any true and adequate understanding of the gospel, and the carefully precise and clear statements about Him which appear in the Creeds and Confessions are evidence of the earnest endeavour of dedicated scholars and teachers to safeguard the Church against misconceptions and views that would lead into heresy.

Nowhere is this seen more critically than in relation to the heart of the Christian Faith, the Atonement. It is here supremely that we see who Christ is, and who He needs to be, in order that atonement can take place at all. On the one hand, atonement, if it is to be a reality, and truly secured, must take place from man's side, for it is man who has sinned against God. On the other hand, however, if it is to be effectual, atonement is something that only God can accomplish, since sin is infinite in its extent and consequences, and can thus be dealt with only by an infinite God.

This is the drama of the divine revelation and intervention in the gospel: atonement requires to come from man's side, and is possible only from God's. This dilemma, if it can be so-called, is resolved once and for all in the mystery of the Incarnation and of the Person of Christ, who unites two natures, divine and human, in Himself. As one of the theologians has put it, 'The background of the atoning deed is not the Godhead *per se,* but the God-manhood of Christ.' As man, in man's life, He accomplishes a real atonement; as God, manifest in our flesh and nature, He makes it truly effectual.

In the history of the Church, sometimes the deity of Christ has been emphasized at the expense of His humanity, and

18

sometimes vice versa. Today, in view of the almost total preoccupation of liberal theology with the human Jesus, and of the common ground that many heretical movements share in derogating from His essential deity, and above all, in the interests of preserving not only a true doctrine of atonement but also the very possibility of one, the true dignity and majesty of the Godhead of the Son needs to be reasserted. And this is what the following readings seek to do.

Editor's note : Volume 7 in this series, while not neglecting the deity of Jesus, emphasizes His humanity, and so the two volumes complement each other.

THE PERSON OF CHRIST

His Deity and Pre-Existence

8 : The Royal Invitation

Matthew 11.20–12.8

The significance of this passage is that it underlines the nature of the controversy between our Lord and the Jewish authorities. It was not His mighty works as such that they objected to, but the claims that were implicit in them. The miracles wrought in Chorazin, Bethsaida and Capernaum were meant to bring about repentance and faith (21–23), the implication being that they were acts of divine power, as was the subsequent pronouncement of woe upon these cities on their refusal to receive His testimony, for who can judge, save God alone?

Our Lord's prayer which follows in v. 25 makes His claim even more explicit, particularly His words in v. 27 which can only be interpreted—as similar teaching was interpreted by the Jews (John 5.16–18)—as the assertion of a unique relationship between Himself and God, that of Sonship. To say that none but the Almighty Father has full knowledge of the mystery of the person and office of the Son, and that none can know the Father except the Son and those to whom the Son reveals Him, is tantamount to His claiming equality with God. It is this that invests the wonderful invitation in vs. 28–30 with such authority and virtue. No mere man could make such an invitation. It echoes the Old Testament appeal, 'Turn to me and be saved, all the ends of the earth', in Isa. 45.22, which is spoken by God Himself.

The same implicit claim lies at the heart of the sabbath controversy in 12.1–8. It is the authoritative re-interpretation of the sabbath law (made in the spirit of the Sermon on the Mount's teaching, 'You have heard that it was said . . . But I say to you', **5**.21 f.) that is so impressive and conclusive here. Not only so: our Lord's assertion that 'something greater than the temple is here' (6) makes what can only be called a superlative claim for Himself. The Temple, for the Jews, enshrined the divine presence, and 'something greater' could only mean that in Him the divine presence was incarnate and visible. And if David had the right to 'violate' the law (1 Sam. **21**) in what he did when he was hungry, how much more had He, who was the great Lawgiver Himself, the Incarnate Son? The Son of man is Lord of the sabbath because He is the Lord.

9 : The Royal Command

Luke 8.22–39

Two miracles are recorded in these verses, the stilling of the storm on the Sea of Galilee, and the healing of the man with the legion of demons. It is commonplace—as it is almost inevitable—to make these stories apply to the storms of life and its torments, and to draw encouragement from them as we face the hazards and difficulties of human experience. But although this is a legitimate application of the miracles, we must not forget that it is true only because something else—and something greater—is true, namely the fact of the Lordship and Kingship of Christ. The point that all three synoptic writers are intent on making in their Gospels is that Jesus, although truly man, is more than mere man, and they present a series of carefully selected miracles and signs with this in view, before finally recording the critical challenge made by our Lord to the disciples at Caesarea Philippi, 'Who do you say that I am?', and Peter's response, 'You are the Christ, the Son of the living God' (Matt. **16**.16). The miracles and signs are meant to elicit such a confession, not only from the disciples, but also from us.

Thus, in the stilling of the storm, Jesus is shown as Lord of nature and the elements, and the disciples 'get the message', saying 'Who then is this, that he commands even wind and water, and they obey him?' (25). No *mere* man could do such a thing; only He who made them could thus control them. In the same way the casting out of the legion of demons shows Jesus as Lord of all dark powers. (We must not make the mistake of equating demon-possession with psychiatric disorder, for the two are not the same. In fact, the Gospel writers sometimes make a clear distinction between the two even when the presenting symptoms are the same in both cases, as a comparison of Matt. **9**.32 f. with Mark **7**.32 and Matt. **15**.30 will show). This claim to Lordship and Deity is implicit in Jesus' words to the healed man, and in his response. He is commanded to return home and declare how much *God* has done for him; he immediately proclaimed how much *Jesus* had done for him. Is not the implication here unavoidable?

10 : The Light of the World

John 8.12–24

The sublime words in v. 12 form a companion with John **7**.37 f., and both refer to the ritual performed at the Feast of Tabernacles, the one to the pouring of water from the Pool of Siloam on the altar by the priests, symbolizing God's provision of water in the wilderness, the other to the illumination of the Temple courts, symbolizing His guidance by the pillar of cloud and fire. Jesus claims to be the fulfilment of both. The claim in v. 12 is therefore a Messianic claim (cf. Isa. **42**.6; **49**.6), and the Pharisees recognize it as such and dispute it. The 'I am' would have deep significance for them, being the Divine Name of the Old Testament (cf. Exod. **3**.14). The discussion that follows shows their need of light. It is His authority that they question and challenge in v. 13. They may be quoting Jesus' own words in **5**.31, 'If I bear witness to myself, my testimony is not true.' If so, this betrays a shallow understanding of His meaning, and a lack of appreciation of who He is. There is no contradiction. Indeed, He goes on to say that His authority and the truth of His witness reside in the fact that He knows where He has come from and where He is going—a clear reference to His eternal Sonship. On this ground He claims the right to be heard.

Something important emerges here: on the one hand, there is, ultimately, no mere rational proof of our Lord's authority; and on the other, once a man perceives His deity, there is no further question of the authority of His words. One does not prove Christ; one believes in Him. The Pharisees were blind to His identity, knowing Him only 'after the flesh.' This is borne out in vs. 16 ff. If they had a mind to believe, there was sufficient 'evidence' on the rational level to satisfy them law-wise (17), for the Father also bore witness to Him (cf. 5.31 ff.), and this fulfils the rabbinic requirement (17 f.). They ask, 'Where is your Father?', not 'Who?' speaking with contempt, thinking His father to be Joseph, the carpenter. But to see no more in Jesus than a human, historical figure, is not to see Him at all. The gulf between them was complete. They understood neither His person nor His work. This was their condemnation and their eternal loss.

11 : The Royal Claim

John 8.25–47

The question 'Who are you?' addressed to Jesus in v. 25 is given an unmistakable answer, for those with ears to hear, in the debate between our Lord and the Jews which occupies the remainder of this chapter. There is only one ground on which the claims implicit in His teaching can be regarded as either credible or free from the charge of blasphemy, namely that of His deity. Jesus' deliberate use of the words 'I am' in v. 28 (there is no 'he' in the original), His claim that continuing in His word means knowing the truth that makes men free (31 f.), and that He can set men truly free (36), His assertion that true children of God will necessarily love Him, the Son, all alike imply and assume His Godhead. Indeed, they do so in such a way that the only real alternative to falling down and worshipping Him was to brand Him as a blasphemer and put Him to death. He did not leave it open either to His hearers or to us to think of Him as only a great religious teacher. It must be the one or the other. There is no intermediate position.

This 'either-or', and the cruciality of His deity for true faith are borne out by a distinction John makes in the two Greek constructions for 'believed' he employs in vs. 30 and 31. From the first we can deduce a faith that involves personal reliance, trust and commitment; from the second, however, in v. 31, we can assume a faith that was merely nominal and superficial, akin to that of certain disciples in 2.23, where we are told that Jesus was not prepared to commit Himself to them. Jesus' words to the Jews that believed in this way have therefore the effect of sifting them, and exposing the fatal lack in their attitude to Him. Hence their immediate reaction in v. 33, objecting to the suggestion that they needed to be made free, and their increasing resistance to His radical probing of their basic attitudes (37, 39). The more He says, the more they reveal their fundamental lack of understanding of the things of God, a blindness due to their unwillingness to receive His testimony concerning Himself (43); until belief in Him that refuses to acknowledge His deity is finally exposed as being of the devil (44). So central is the doctrine of the deity of Christ for true, saving faith.

12 : The Eternal Christ

John 8.48–59

The accusation of demon-possession levelled against Jesus in these verses marks a climax in the conflict between Jesus and His critics, and exposes the depth of their unbelief and their inability to receive His testimony concerning Himself. One thing is clear, not only from these verses, but also from those which precede them: the Jews were in no doubt as to the kind of claim Jesus was making for Himself. They knew He was claiming Messiahship and Deity; and since such a claim to Deity was unthinkable, the only possible alternative must be that He had a devil. Only one who was either devil-possessed or the Messiah could dare to speak as Jesus does in v. 51. This is what lies behind the contemptuous question they ask in v. 53, 'Are you greater than our father Abraham?' To this Jesus answers two things: firstly, that Abraham 'rejoiced that he was to see my day; he saw it and was glad.' Jesus means and implies that Abraham's faith looked forward to His own coming, and indeed rested upon that coming; and by implication He indicates that the faith of all the old dispensation was faith in the promise of His coming. Secondly, He uttered perhaps the most profound of all His statements, 'Before Abraham was, I am.' These words not only serve to reinforce the earlier claim in v. 56, making even more explicit His pre-existence, but also in the use of the sacred 'I am' emphasize His eternal pre-existence and His essential Deity. This assumption of the divine Name of the Old Testament could lead only to worship and adoration, on the part of those who believed in Him, and the assumption of blasphemy, on the part of those who did not. It was on this ground that they took up stones to throw at Him (59).

13 : Jesus—Word of God Incarnate

John 1.1–5; 20.19–29

The association of ideas in these two passages, one from the prologue of John's Gospel, the other from the Resurrection narratives, is considerable, and serves to underline John's essential message. For one thing, in what is perhaps the most sublime passage in the New Testament, the apostle identifies the One of whom he is to write and speak as being the eternal Word by whom all things were made. This is He, the light and life of men, who was made flesh (1.14), and entered into death and passed through it to victory 'for us men and for our salvation.' It is when we view the death of Christ in this light that we see, as Peter made plain on the day of Pentecost (Acts 2.24), that death could not hold Him, but had to concede the victory to Him. It was the eternal Son who entered into death: it could not but be abolished, bringing to birth a gospel of life and immortality. The darkness could not overcome the light that had invaded it (1.5).

This is the significance of the risen Christ's words to the disciples in **20**.19, 21, 'Peace be with you'. There was now nothing left, death being vanquished, to prevent or disturb their peace. John may have had the original creation story in mind when writing these words, for, as in the beginning, the sabbath rest and peace of God were disturbed by the entrance of sin, so here peace is restored by the Creator-Redeemer God. Also, on the first day of creation God said, 'Let there be light', and there was light; and now, on the first day of the week—the first day of the new creation, so to speak— light came once again to the disciples: 'Then the disciples were glad when they saw the Lord' (**20**.20).

In this context, the episode of Thomas's doubt is seen to be without excuse. If Christ be the eternal Son who has become incarnate and passed through death, His risen, victorious Presence really commands belief and trust. And Thomas, when he realizes the truth of the situation, emerges from doubt into true faith, confessing Christ as his Lord and his God. This is the logical, inevitable conclusion to which John's Gospel is designed to lead us. In the light of this fact how impossible becomes the translation of **1**.1 ('The Word was a god') advanced by the Jehovah's Witnesses! It does justice neither to the grammar of the Greek (see the larger commentaries for the technicalities), nor to the place of the statement in a Gospel which leads up to the great confession of Thomas.

14 : The Mighty Indwelling

Colossians 1.9–23

Paul's prayer in vs. 9–12a that the Colossians would lead a life worthy of the Lord follows the usual apostolic pattern of basing exhortations to holiness and fruitfulness on the doctrines of the faith. Ethical imperatives rest on the indicatives of grace which are their inspiration and dynamic. Here, these indicatives concern the person and work of Christ. Every phrase in the sustained theological treatment of this theme is charged with deep significance. Christ is the image of the invisible God (15). He both represents and manifests the Father, not merely in His pre-incarnate existence as the second Person of the Trinity, but also in His existence now as the glorified Lord in heaven. He is also the first-born of all creation. This does not mean that He was the first of the created beings. He was not created at all, as v. 17 makes clear. The NEB and J. B. Phillips both capture the real sense when they say 'His is the primacy over all created things' (NEB) and 'He existed before creation began' (J. B. Phillips). Priority and sovereignty over all creation is what is meant, and this is expanded in vs. 16 and 17. 'He is both the first principle and the upholding principle of the whole scheme of creation' (J. B. Phillips).

The particular aspect of Christ's redeeming work that Paul emphasizes here is reconciliation. Two points in particular must be underlined. First of all, Paul says that this reconciling Christ is the great Creator Himself. The work of reconciliation is so vast and infinite that only One who was God could accomplish it. No one who was less could ever have done what Jesus did. For reconciliation is the putting away by God of God's own condemnation of the world and its sin, and its message is that the awful barrier between man and God has been removed once for all by an awful demonstration of divine love, by God Himself, in the Person of His Son. Secondly, Paul places this message of man's reconciliation in a larger, vaster context—the reconciliation of 'all things, whether on earth or in heaven' (20). It is this universal cosmic reconciliation in which man shares, and of which his is a part, albeit the significant and decisive part. Well might Paul exclaim that such a Christ is pre-eminent and that 'in Him all the fullness of God was pleased to dwell'!

15 : God's Last Word to Men

Hebrews 1.1–2.4

The theme of Hebrews is the excellency of Christ, and His superiority to everything in Judaism. The opening statement (1 f.) is one of the most majestic utterances in all Scripture, sounding out like the movement of a great symphony and, symphony-wise, announcing the principal subject matter of all that follows. The writer contrasts how God spoke 'of old' —in shadows, in illustrations, in the law, in history, through the prophets—with how He has spoken 'in these last days' in Christ. In none of the former was His full revelation given, and something still remained to be said. Christ is God's last word to man, for in Him He answers all the need of humanity.

This Son in whom God has spoken is described in language that stresses His unique, solitary excellence. He is 'heir of all things' (1.2), that is, everything in creation exists for Him, a stupendous claim forcing us to conclude that He could not have been a mere created being, but One who is eternal (and consequently immeasurably superior to angels, who are created beings). Thus we come to the thought of His involvement in creation itself—'through whom also he created the world'. 'Before Abraham was, I am,' Christ once said, and He could have said as truly, 'Before creation was, I am.' The force of the description of Christ in v. 3a lies in the significance it gives to what follows in v. 3b, as if to say, 'It took such an One as this eternal, all-glorious One, who is God the Son, to deal with sin.' It is this mighty work, including within its compass the resurrection and ascension, that constitutes God's word to men. It is a word of pardon and salvation that He speaks in Christ.

The rest of the chapter establishes the superiority of Christ, and the revelation given in Him, over the angels. The old Arian doctrine of the 4th century and the teaching of modern Jehovah's Witnesses and Christadelphians virtually reduces the pre-incarnate Christ to a kind of super-angel. For our writer, however, they are servants, He is the Son (4–6); they are subjects, He is the King who reigns over them (7–9); they are creatures, He is Creator (10-14). And by virtue of His victory He has been elevated to His superlative position at the right hand of God, and towers over the created order as its King and Head. Hence the warning in 2.1–4. If the message declared by angels was worthy of serious attention, how much more the message of the King of angels, in whom such a great salvation is proclaimed to men?

Questions and themes for study and discussion on Studies 8–15

1. Is it the greatness of man's need, or the authority in the invitation in Matt. 11.28, that constrains him to come to Christ?

2. On the evidence given in Luke 8.22–39 what do *we* think of Christ?

3. How does Paul's statement in 2 Cor. 5.16 help us to understand the Jews' attitude in John 8.12–24?

4. What are the marks of true faith, according to the teaching of John 8.25–47?

5. Jesus said Abraham saw His day (John 8.56), yet the Jews in reply spoke of His seeing Abraham. Why did they turn the statement round? Did they really understand what He meant?

6. How does John show (John 20.19–29) that the darkness (1.5) has not overcome the light?

7. How does Paul's teaching in Col. 1.9–23 compare with John's in the prologue to his Gospel?

8. How does the teaching of Heb. 1 compare with that of Paul and John?

9. Is there really any value in saying we accept the authority of the Bible if we evade its teaching as to the deity of Jesus, as Jehovah's Witnesses and others do?

CHARACTER STUDIES

16 : The Damaged Exiles

Psalm 137; Romans 12.14

It is possible that the strange problem of at least one of the Imprecatory Psalms finds its explanation here. Was Psa. **137** included, under God's overruling, in the Psalter for the same reasons as the Book of Esther—to reveal the mind and fate of those who were crushed, broken and embittered under persecution? Perhaps among the characters of the Bible we should number the group 'by the waters of Babylon'.

The little poem begins gently, showing the exiles meeting, as the exiles did, by the willow-hung river (cf. Acts **16**.13). A crowd gathered menacingly around, saw their musical instruments, and called for a song. The tiny band was in no mood for singing to entertain those who had caused their pain. They had no defence save that of 'commination'. There is a Form of Commination, seldom if ever used, in the Anglican Prayer Book, and in an Eastern context such a ritual curse could be the only weapon available in a menacing situation. The psalm is a drama. The first verses show a picture of Jewish worshippers meeting in peace, the gathering of threat and peril, and then, without intervening preamble, the fierce words of denunciation by which they sought to protect their lives from the savage mob, invoking on the Chaldaean crowd the very horrors which they, or their soldiers, had inflicted in the streets of Jerusalem.

When the distinguished Arabic scholar, Professor E. H. Palmer, was murdered by Arab bandits in Sinai in 1882, he sought to save his life by this very means. He had a deep knowledge of the wild Bedouin, and his friends were shocked to hear that he had solemnly cursed them before he died.

In his hands, though finally unavailing, the curse was a formidable weapon of defence. A curse to an Oriental is a solemn and an awful thing. It is loaded with foreboding, lies like lead on a guilty mind, and goes with a criminal like a demon to haunt the silence, fill the night, and sometimes to madden and to kill.

Palmer failed. The pathetic exiles under the willows may, by the same dire means, have saved their lives. But here is light on Esther. She carried into action, thanks to her royal position, the comminations of the exiles of Psa. 137. Nor was the pogrom of the Jews against the Gentiles an unexampled phenomenon. Such vengeance precipitated minor civil war more than once in the early Roman Empire.

17 : The Anthologist

Psalm 119.1–56

If we carefully comb the later psalms, it seems possible to see some of the Jews of the Exile. Book 5 of the psalms is different from all the rest. One can almost see the working of the mind of the man who put the collection together. He had several small collections to hand, the Egyptian Hallel, as it was called (Pss. 113–118) and the Great Hallel (Pss. 120–136). Within these collections lay 'the Songs of Ascent' (Pss. 120–134). Book 5 of the psalms was by way of being the hymn-book of the second Temple, built after the Exile.

The man who put this collection together, adding to the smaller collections some psalms of David which had not been included in the first four books, but which had meant much to him personally, decided, perhaps, that he would divide the book neatly into two by a collection of his own. Hence the longest of all the psalms—Psa. 119. At some time in his life, the word of God had meant all to him, and could this have been at any more likely time than during the Exile, when the devout among the troubled Jews, cut off from all the worship and ritual of the Temple, turned with fervour to the Word? If our interpretation is correct, our anthologist collected from all quarters sayings about the Word of God. Some of the mass of sayings he no doubt wrote himself. He arranged them in groups of eight, under all the twenty-two letters of the Hebrew alphabet, to make it simpler to memorize them. He arranged them round certain central thoughts, or developing processes of thought, and it is a study of some delicacy to read Psa. 119 until the patterns of its thought become real and meaningful.

In the same process we get to know the anthologist. It is fairly clear that he was the author of Psa. 1, and so must have been the senior rabbi in charge of the collection and ordering of the Psalter. The putting together, in reverence, of the ancient Scriptures which had meant so much to them in the days of exile must have been an immediate and absorbing task, when the nation began its new struggle to rebuild in the shattered homeland. Their work has not been studied closely enough to discover the reasons for their groupings, the patterns of thought, the relation of that thought to possible experience. Here at any rate we have one of the men involved. We shall spend another day in trying to see him.

18 : The Anthologist Again

Psalm 119.57–96

Taking parts, portions, verses of the collector's mass of sayings about the Word, we may make some guesses about him and the experiences he had endured. Imagination, to be sure, but imagination under some rigour of discipline can be a pathway to better understanding!

Look closely at this long psalm. The collector of the choice sayings had known persecution (22, 23); he had suffered under the heavy or the ruthless hand of authority (61, 69). Was this in Babylon, or in Babylon's successor in despotism, that of Persia? Under the burden of it all his faith had staggered (6, 22, 31), and there was such pressure to give in and conform, such pressure as Daniel and his friends must have known (36, 37). As Mordecai has revealed to us, in material things, the great empire and its affluent cities offered tempting advantages to the covetous. The Jews were a clever people, and it is obvious that the ruins of Jerusalem and their downtrodden land were not attractive to the worldly-minded. But our anthologist, busy collecting his book of sayings, was a true man, and he was grieved that he should be so tempted. His own wavering concerned him.

His long psalm is a fascinating study. He was very pre-occupied with happiness, and he made this his theme in Psa. 1 if the assumption that he wrote it is correct. Observe his first eight verses. Verses 1 and 2 speak of true happiness; vs. 3 and 4 attach happiness to steadfastness; but such is life, that they only can be steadfast who are healthily aware of the danger of falling (5, 6). And that danger is diminished by remembering the life's once-for-all committal (7, 8), and one's vows to the Most High.

The third section (gimel) seems curiously autobiographical. The anthologist had known deprivation and fear for his life (17), the dryness of soul which finds no beauty in the Word (18), loneliness and rejection (19), stress and tension ('My soul yearns all the time for thee to intervene'—Moffatt, 20). He sees hope glimmer in answer to his prayer (21), and claims the rewards of steadfastness—he has 'kept the faith' (22), even in the face of powerful contempt (23), for where else is guidance (24)?

19 : Man of Obedience

Psalm 119.97–152

The 'whole heart' is a preoccupation with the Jew we seek to know (e.g. 34, 58, 69, 145). We know that all good lightly held can slip out of the hands. He was aware that half-hearted virtue is soon no virtue at all. He was conscious that what God called for was the dedication of the whole personality. Truth must be held 'in the inward being' (Psa. 51.6) to be held at all, and all thought, speech, conduct was ultimately determined by that which dwells in the core of the personality.

He knew, too, that the fundamental virtue was obedience—

the obverse of the fundamental sin, pride, which involves disobedience, the assertion of the self, the human will, against God. How basic is the lesson the anthologist had learned as he studied the Word 'by the waters of Babylon'! Obedience is the theme of the whole Bible, and a determinant factor in personality after personality of the scores we have studied during these two years. Look at Matt. 7.21, Rom. 5.21—6.2. And consider the very opening scene of the Bible in Eden.

'The first law that ever God gave to man', said the French essayist, Michel Montaigne, four centuries ago, 'was the law of obedience. It was a commandment pure and simple, wherein man had nothing to enquire after or dispute, forasmuch as to obey is the proper office of a rational soul acknowledging a heavenly superior and benefactor.' And it was another Frenchman, a century later, the great preacher, Jacques Bossuet, who remarked simply: 'Thirty years of our Lord's life are hidden in those words of the Gospel—"He was subject to them".'

Pick verses from the psalm supporting this. The anthologist had learned a deep and basic truth, that, contrary to common opinion, command is anxiety, and obedience is peace, and that obedience to truth revealed to us is the royal and certain path to the understanding of wider truth which lies beyond the horizon of the mind. After all, if God be the end and object of our obedience, is obedience anything more than submission of the helpless soul to Love, Wisdom and Strength? That is why the anthologist came back to Jerusalem when Ezra and Nehemiah showed the way. That great movement will soon be our theme.

20 : The Happy Man

Psalm 1; 119.153–176

Psa. 1 is probably the last psalm to be written in the whole Psalter. It is designed to introduce the whole book, which begins, like the ministry of Christ, with defining the truly happy man. This is a preoccupation of the writer, but it is the ideal and abstract character who will be in our thoughts in this study, and we have little to do but reconstruct, in more modern language, the picture.

But take a last look at the author. He revered the Word, and knew that the task he now undertook was to introduce a book of that Word, a song-book of God's people. Hebrew poetry was based on parallelism of ideas and the writer was a poet. But how he now extended himself and poured his best gifts into the psalm! The whole psalm is a contrast of good and evil in man, but in the first verse he develops a word pattern of three times three: walks, counsel, wicked; stands, way, sinners; sits, seat, scoffers. And more, not only is the ninefold word-structure ornamental, it is also true to spiritual truth, and reveals the process of backsliding which he had combated in his own experience.

Who is the happy man? Listen to him: 'He is a happy man who never allows his course of life to be dictated by what those think who take no thought of God.' And is it not a fact that true servants of God must resist public opinion, and reject many social trends and thought patterns of their day?

And 'he is a happy man who does not find his chief pleasure in the company of those who care nothing for God's laws.' Finally, 'he is a happy man who does not adopt the way of life of those who hold God in contempt'—but 'who, in his whole manner of life, seeks to do God's will, who finds pleasure in the company of God's people, and who seeks to live as those live who honour Him.'

Such people hold eroding society together, like the trees whose clinging roots hold the crumbling soil of a denuded hill when the freshets of man's greedy devising tear the fertile soil away. Observe the point which Jeremiah adds (**17**.8)—'reaching its roots to the water.' To be such a child of God calls for a conscious reaching for Him, a constant feeding on His nourishment and strength.

Questions and themes for study and discussion on Studies 16–20

1. What should be the place of the Word in our devotional life?
2. Memorizing Scripture.

3. The nature of true happiness.
4. How well did the writer of Psa. **119** know the rest of the Psalter? Can you discover echoes?
5. Why is obedience important? See Rom. **12**.1 f.
6. Describe 'the heart'.
7. 'To be happy is not the purpose of our lives, but to deserve happiness' (Fichte).

THE PERSON OF CHRIST

His Incarnation and Virgin Birth

21 : Immanuel—God with Us

Isaiah 7.1–17

The reference to Immanuel in this prophecy needs to be understood in its historical context, which is unfolded in 2 Kings 16.1–9. Syria and Israel have entered into a coalition against Judah, and Isaiah exhorts Ahaz to trust in the Lord, and to appeal for help to Assyria. Seeing, however, that the king was not disposed to take his advice, he appealed to him to seek a sign from the Lord. But Ahaz, knowing that any sign from God must simply confirm Isaiah's word to him, refuses to do so, whereupon Isaiah announces that God would give him a sign. On one interpretation this was a sign of judgement instead of grace. The sign would be simple enough to interpret but for the name Immanuel involved in it. A child born of a virgin was to be the divine sign, and by the time he was come to years of discretion he would be eating curds and honey, which, on this interpretation, was the food of privation and desolation, of a people whose land, depopulated by the enemy, had been turned into pasture. In a matter of a few years, Syria and Ephraim were to be laid waste and Judah made desolate. But why should the wonderful name Immanuel, God with us, be associated with judgement, when it is so inseparably associated with the promised Messiah? The link is this: the child would become an innocent Sufferer, a Man of sorrows. There is a marvellously mysterious interweaving of events here to produce the picture of a suffering Servant. G. Adam Smith refers to Ahaz

37

as the Judas of the Old Testament, who sells the Messiah by wilfully seeking to bring about the kingdom in his own sinful way. The name Immanuel, God with us, must surely have pointed the true way to Ahaz. Trust in Him, cried Isaiah, not in Assyria. But Ahaz was intent on going his own way, and as such stands as the symbol of a people of God whose continued faithlessness caused the Christ to be born into a subject race. Here is the beginning of the rejection of the Messiah by a people who knew not the time of their visitation. The sign may well have found its immediate fulfilment in one whose mother was still a virgin when the prophecy was given, but it reaches out beyond him to a greater than he. And the instinct of the New Testament Church was right when it saw in these words a Messianic hope and regarded them as fulfilled in the birth of Christ.

22 : The Virgin Birth of Christ

Matthew 1.18–25

The essential point that Matthew makes here is that there was something uniquely special and different about the birth of Jesus. What is the mystery of the virgin birth meant to teach us? It is not simply that it was necessary in order to ensure that Jesus would be sinless, not partaking of the heritage and taint of sin through Joseph—for would not the taint have been inherited equally through Mary? Rather, the mystery and the miracle lie in this, that in the divine provision of salvation man, as man, is completely set aside. 'The male, as the specific agent of human action and history, with his responsibility for directing the human species, must now retire into the background, as the powerless figure of Joseph' (Barth). It is this setting aside of man as such that is the real heart of the biblical testimony, and it tells us that that part in us that wants to do, and indeed insists on doing, something active for our own salvation is resolutely and firmly set aside by God. Salvation is of God, and all of grace.

Furthermore, the doctrine declares unequivocally that here, in Jesus Christ, God is beginning a new thing. Matthew has already hinted at this in the phrase 'the book of the genealogy of Jesus Christ' (1.1), which echoes similar phrases in Gen. 2.4 and 5.1 about the 'generations of Adam', as if to suggest that as Genesis tells the story of the tragic fall of the first Adam, so now he is to tell the story of the second Adam which is the divine answer to man's need. This becomes even more explicit in the statement that Mary was found to be with child of the Holy Spirit, for this perhaps echoes Gen. 1.2, where 'the Spirit of God was moving over the face of the waters'. Here, then, was an act of new creation. The old humanity, in spite of its glory and promise, had come to grief, and now the new humanity, signifying a complete break with the old, and a new beginning, was being ushered in. And as by its sin the old humanity had been cut off from God, so now the new order was to be characterized by a reversal of this tragedy. God had come to men once more—Emmanuel, God with us.

23 : The Divine Visitation

Luke 1.26–45

Luke's account of the virgin birth of Christ takes us behind what Matthew tells us to the manner in which our Lord's birth came about. The passage contains three lessons of enormous significance. First is the fact of the divine visitation. The angel Gabriel comes to Mary to announce the Saviour's birth. It is a moment of destiny in which the sovereign Lord of the universe approaches His creature, bestowing on her the unique privilege of becoming the mother of the Saviour of the world. All Old Testament history is summed up in this confrontation—through the primal work of creation, the experiences of Abraham, the wilderness wanderings, Judah's and Israel's backslidings, and the turmoil of the Captivity, God had His eyes steadily fixed on this encounter; and all His dealings with His people were designed to lead to this crucial moment. As Paul says, the time had fully come (Gal. 4.4). Mary's question 'How?' in v. 34 underlines the mystery we also feel here, and the angel's answer tells us as much as we shall ever understand. The birth was to be a divine visitation, and the Spirit of God was to overshadow her, as that Spirit had once brooded upon the face of the deep in the beginning of creation, to create in her this unique Life that was to be the life of men.

The second lesson lies in Mary's response to the message of the angel. Two things are said about this. On the one hand, Elizabeth speaks of Mary's confidence that the promise given her would be fulfilled (45). Her response to the angelic annunciation was one of true faith. But, on the other, faith for her meant submitting to the word of the Lord, abandoning herself to it and to its power in her life (38). And her blessedness (45) consisted in that, having been chosen for this special service, and having received an amazing promise, she rose unreservedly to the summons of God in obedience and submission.

Finally, the angel's words in v. 35 beautifully illustrate what has been called 'the virgin birth of faith in the soul'. What the angel said would happen to Mary also happens to men through the preaching of the Word. This is how men are born of the Spirit; and the newness of life they receive is the coming of the Christ to dwell in their hearts.

24 : God Manifest in the Flesh

John 1.6–18

The central affirmation that John makes concerning the Incarnation is that it is the eternal Word, by whom the worlds were made, that became flesh in the Babe of Bethlehem, and dwelt among us. It will be enough, in studying this passage, to try to understand something of the meaning of this astounding statement.

What does John mean to convey by saying that the Word became flesh? He does not, and cannot, mean that He ceased to be what He was before, and became something else, as the more extreme 'Kenosis' theologians maintained. He did not cease to be God, although He became man. To say that He came in disguise, incognito, conveys something of the mystery,

40

(although in another sense this is just as misleading). Behind the disguise there is the Person of God the Son. He it is who is come in the flesh (1 John **4**.2), not another, and when Paul speaks of His emptying Himself (Phil. **2**.7), that self-emptying must be understood as the laying aside of the *mode* of divine existence which He enjoyed with the Father, not the laying aside of what He was, and is. He became a servant but there was never a moment, not even in the manger, when He ceased to be God. The idea of a disguise, however, is misleading in that, for us, a disguise is something we dispense with when it is no longer needed. But Jesus Christ does not lay aside His human 'disguise'. He has become man for ever. 'Manhood taken by the Son' was not a temporary expedient, but something done once for all and for ever. It is the permanent hallowing and sanctifying of humanity.

On the other hand, the word 'flesh' must be taken with real seriousness. God the Son really became man. The humanity of Christ was, and is, real and complete. He was, and is, fully and permanently man. This is mystery indeed, but the mystery must be accepted. Jesus is divine and Jesus is human, both God and man. He has two natures, the divine and the human, united in one Person, the God-man. The Word is not made flesh by changing one nature into another, or by laying aside one nature and taking up another, but by the Godhead taking manhood. To grasp this fact is to be delivered from much heretical thinking, both ancient and modern. The Incarnation is the mystery of God manifest in the flesh.

25 : The Mystery of Godliness

1 Timothy 3.14–4.6

This passage contains one of the richest expressions of Christian truth in existence (3.16). Many scholars think it is a quotation from an ancient credal hymn in use in the early Church. The form of the sixfold statement suggests a hymnal construction, falling into two parts or 'verses', the first describing the life of the incarnate Son of God on earth, the second the life of the glorified Lord in heaven. (Incidentally, 'the mystery of our religion' (RSV) means 'the open secret of our piety', and refers to Christ Himself (cf. Eph. 3.4). The passage speaks of the Incarnation but the RSV omits the word 'God' on textual grounds.)

Paul's words 'He was manifested in the flesh' are a direct equivalent of John 1.1–14. The eternal Word became man, coming from beyond time into time for our sakes. This clearly implies Christ's pre-existence before Bethlehem, but also proclaims that the human Jesus was the divine, eternal Son. Christ remained God the Son when He became man. Some take 'vindicated in the Spirit' to refer to the whole of Christ's earthly life and work being borne testimony to by the Spirit; others, to the resurrection, by which he was 'designated Son of God in power' (Rom. 1.4); others, as covering the whole of biblical revelation, including the testimony of the Spirit to Him in Old Testament days—i.e. in prophecy, in His earthly life, and finally in His resurrection. 'Seen of angels' is a striking concept, suggesting the wonder and awe with which the angels of God viewed the unfolding mystery of the Incarnation.

'Preached among the nations' sums up the whole of the Acts, and indeed all Church history. It was for this that the divine promise in Christ's life, death and resurrection was fulfilled, that there might be a gospel to preach to all men. The grandeur of Paul's thought here thrills the heart. While the angelic world was admiring on high the matchless grace of God, the world of men below was hearing and responding to the glad sound of the gospel. This is the force of 'believed on in the world'. Faith comes by hearing, and the power of the self-manifestation of God is such that it bends the wills and reconciles the hearts of men to Himself. 'Taken up in glory' speaks of Christ's 'official' appointment to the place of power and authority as Victor over sin and death and hell. It is His coronation, on the basis of which He exercises His kingly rule and ministers the benefits of His earthly mediatorial work to men. Great, indeed, is the mystery of our religion!

26 : Born to Die

Hebrews 2.5–18

These verses unfold the meaning and purpose of our Lord's Incarnation. The writer's concern is to reconcile the fact that Jesus is immeasurably superior to the angels (1.4) with the apparently incongruous fact of His being a man who died in shame and ignominy. The argument from Psa. 8 is that it is a prediction of 'the world to come', and is saying that man, though reduced for a period of time below the level of the angels, is yet destined to occupy the highest place among God's creatures, and that this transformation is accomplished by our Lord's becoming man. Thus, He is made for a little while lower than the angels (v. 9), He becomes our brother (v. 11), He partakes of our nature (v. 14), He is made like His brethren in every respect (v. 17). It is His being made man that qualifies Him for this task, but it is not simply by becoming man that He fulfils it. Rather, He became man in order to die (for God is deathless and so are angels), and it is by His death that He accomplishes man's redemption and secures to him his ultimate destiny in the world to come.

The writer makes three statements about the death of Christ, each being represented as fulfilling the purpose of His having become man. The first, in v. 9, speaks of His having tasted death for everyone. Death here is not simply death as we know it, but death as the wages of sin, and Jesus drank that cup to its bitter dregs, that we might never have to do so. The second statement, in v. 14, claims that through death Christ destroyed him who has the power of death, that is, the devil. The death He died was the battle-ground on which He grappled with and conquered the dark powers that lie behind the woes of man, destroying them, not in the sense of putting them out of existence, but of robbing them of their power over man. The third statement, v. 17, speaks of Christ making expiation for the sins of the people. The word in the Greek is better translated 'propitiation', and speaks of the controversy that sin has raised between God and man, and the turning away of the divine anger by the atoning blood of the Mediator. For all this, the Son of God became incarnate.

27 : The Godhead of the Son

1 John 1.1–4; 4.1–6

The opening words of John's Epistle deal with the same subject as the Prologue to his Gospel, namely the eternal pre-existence and historical manifestation of the Son of God. The apostle's assertion is that the Eternal, the Invisible, the Intangible, has been manifested in a historical Incarnation in such a way that men could hear, see and handle it. The underlying presupposition of all his teaching is the breaking in from beyond of the Power behind all power, a super-natural visitation that conditions all existence, for weal or woe. In this categorical statement, John effectively demolishes the contentions of the heretics of his day, the false prophets of 4.1. It is the Eternal Son, none other, who has been incarnate in history, the Eternal God who has entered time in the person of Jesus. He who is from the beginning is one and the same as He whom the apostles heard, saw and handled. It is impossible, John implies, to distinguish as the heretics did, between the historical Jesus and the eternal Christ, for the Eternal Son *is* Jesus, and He came down *to be seen* of men. It is impossible, therefore, for them to say that the Incarnation was only a seeming one, and that the 'Christ' came upon Jesus only at His baptism and left Him before He died on the cross. This heresy is known as Docetism (from the Greek *dokein* 'to seem to be'). Any conception of our Lord's person which does not take His humanity seriously may be broadly defined as 'docetic'. For a man to deny that Jesus Christ is come in the flesh, means that he is not of God, but of the devil (4.3).

Such is the apostolic proclamation (1.3); and the grand aim it has in view is that through this incomparable message men may be restored to fellowship—with God and with His Son Jesus Christ and, through them, with all the company of the faithful—and brought into fullness of joy (1.4). In thus summing up the essence of the meaning of the gospel, John shows the absolute cruciality of the Incarnation, and pro-vides a standard or norm by which to assess the worth of any man's message. 'Put them to this test,' he says. 'If they do not confess the Godhead of the Son, they are not of God.' It is as simple as that. If Jesus is not God manifest in the flesh, there is no gospel, no true atonement, and no forgiveness of sins.

28 : Christ is Victor

Revelation 12

The book of Revelation divides naturally into two parts, chs. **1–11** and **12–22**. In the first, the main theme is the conflict between the Church and the world, in the second, we are shown that that conflict is the outward manifestation of the war between Christ and the powers of darkness. The world and the hearts of men are the battleground of spiritual forces striving for the victory. Here we have the picture of a dragon standing before a woman about to give birth to a child, ready to destroy it. The child is born, and is caught up to God and His throne. The woman flees to the wilderness, where God has prepared for her food and shelter (1–6). Then (7–12) we see war in heaven, and the dragon is cast from heaven to earth. The dragon immediately persecutes the woman (13–17) and she experiences the care and protection of God.

The child in this symbolic picture is Christ, and the testimony of John's words is that the fundamental battle between good and evil in the universe centres upon Him. The woman symbolizes the one people of God throughout the ages, the Israel of God from whom the promised Messiah comes. This, therefore, is a pictorial representation of the Incarnation, a telescopic picture of the history of the Old Testament revelation culminating in the fulfilment of the promise made in the Garden of Eden (Gen. 3.15). Christ is the promised Seed, born to do battle with the dragon, that old serpent the devil. But Christ's work of redemption is not accomplished through the Incarnation alone: He is 'caught up to God and to His throne' (5), a clear reference to His ascension, which completed the 'movement' begun by His coming down to earth for our sakes. The consequences of this are described in vs. 7–12: Satan as accuser of the brethren is cast out, and is no longer able to bring any charge against God's elect (Rom. 8.33). It is this that constitutes victory for the people of God, and is the ultimate purpose of the Incarnation, a purpose which not all Satan's pressures and attacks can avail to frustrate (13–17). They may be 'killed all the day long' as the chapter indicates, but in all these things they will be 'more than conquerors through him who loved us' (Rom. **8**.36 f.).

Questions and themes for study and discussion on Studies 21–28

1. How does the 'child' in Isa. **7** illustrate the Pauline statement that 'God chose what is weak in the world to shame the strong'?

2. What is Matthew's purpose in linking the birth of Jesus with the Old Testament prophecies?

3. What does Luke's account of the Annunciation have to tell us about the nature and reward of faith?

4. Could Christ fully make God known to men if He were not wholly divine as well as truly human?

5. What does 1 Tim. **3**.16 reveal about the early Church's grasp of Christ's 'finished work'?

6. What does Heb. **2**.5–18 tell us about the relation between the Incarnation and the Atonement?

7. Why is the Deity of Christ (1 John **1**.1–4) so essential for the very existence of the gospel?

8. What does Rev. **12** tell us about the nature of Christ's victory on the cross?

CHARACTER STUDIES

29 : Cyrus the King

Ezra 1.1–2.2, 61–70

Cyrus is a name only in Scripture, but he is known in secular history especially among the Greeks. The dramatist Aeschylus speaks of him with reverence, Herodotus tells of his contacts with the West in his Third Book, and Xenophon uses him as an idealized figure in a treatise on education. In Ezra, Cyrus appears as the author of the decree of liberation which restored the Jews to their native land and permitted the restoration of the Temple worship. This was in 538 B.C., one year after Cyrus captured Babylon.

Cyrus was a founder of empire, the Persian Augustus. He was a genius, and a humane man. It is only characters remarkable in their own right who are idealized, and made a theme of anecdote and legend, as Cyrus was by both Jew and Greek. It was part of Cyrus' wisdom to dismantle the megalomaniac schemes of Nebuchadnezzar's Babylon. He saw both the folly of retaining against their will in the heartland of empire restless minorities, who could only form pabulum and raw material for disaffection, and the parallel advantage of re-establishing on the frontiers of his empire loyal communities indebted to him for their restoration and revival.

These sound political reasons formed sufficient motive for Cyrus, quite apart from any sympathy with the Jews' monotheism, which no doubt appealed to the Persians' view of God more immediately than the complicated paganism of the Babylonians. Whatever the motive, the faith of Jeremiah was finding justification. History was not out of control. God was working out His purposes. Jeremiah's vision of the seventy years (**25**.12) was finding accomplishment, and no knowledge

47

by the Persian ruler of those oracles was needed for the wheels of destiny to move.

Cyrus' character is shown in his decree. It is marked by generosity, adequate provision for the very considerable expense involved in reconstituting a centre of worship and nationhood, and by a liberal spirit. No Jew was compelled to return to the shattered homeland. Many did not. A third generation was growing up in a world to which the Jew had become accustomed. The call had to be real, and obedience sacrificial, when Cyrus' decree was promulgated, to stir ancient longings in the hearts of good men (5).

30 : Zerubbabel

Ezra 3 and 4; Psalm 126

The leader of the second Exodus is a figure almost as shadowy as his companion, appropriately enough a second Joshua. It is often our task in these studies to seek a character, a personality, rather in the events with which their lives were twined than in any word-picture of the historian. Indeed, it is probably the matter-of-fact writer of Chronicles who writes much of the Book of Ezra. Observe how the end of one book forms the beginning of the other.

Zerubbabel must have been a noble man. He faced deprivation and sacrifice, for he was of royal blood, son of Shealtiel, grandson of Jehoiachin (Matt. 1.12), and as such likely to be of standing, even in the land of the alien. A considerable caravan went with Zerubbabel, and their number must have included, like Gideon's remnant, the truest of the land.

The Jews sensed some awkwardness over the division between those who stayed behind and those who faced the sacrifice, and, like the Pilgrim Fathers, and more than one group of colonists, returned to toil, sweat, and tears. The Talmud crudely suggests, in one place, that it was the chaff which returned to Jerusalem, while the wheat remained, and it is possible that the pilgrims and their leader faced some opposition from those who stayed by the fleshpots. They may have marched with much misgiving, and much stress of soul.

And, as we have seen the Book of Esther teach, God's provident care did not desert those who chose the easier road. After all, the families of Ezra and Nehemiah were among their number, for eighty years slipped by after Zerubbabel before those two patriots marched south.

Picture Zerubbabel, then, as another man who knew how to stand alone. It is one of life's most vital lessons. J. R. Lowell, the nineteenth-century American poet, was right:

> *Count me o'er earth's chosen heroes—they were*
> *souls that stood alone,*
> *While the men they agonized for hurled the*
> *contumelious stone;*
> *Stood serene and down the future saw the golden*
> *beam incline*
> *To the side of perfect justice . . . and to God's supreme*
> *design.*

31 : Haggai the Prophet

Ezra 5.1–5; Haggai 1.1–2.9

Haggai, like the other prophet of his day, Zechariah, seems to have been active about 520 B.C. It is a fair guess that both men came back to Judea as children along with Zerubbabel's caravan. There is the ardour of young manhood in Haggai's preaching, for his small book seems no more than excerpts from notable sermons preached to a community whose hands had wearied under the hardships of the restoration. Those early days must have been difficult.

Perhaps an ecstatic memory of early childhood was the sound of mingled joy and weeping (Ezra 3.12, 13), when the first stones and timber of the new Temple were visible. But the building lagged. The people, who had endured much of the rain and the cold in the early days of their return to the devastated land, had now their soundly roofed houses (1.4) and it would be difficult to grudge those settlers and pioneers this small alleviation of the arduous conditions under which they had begun their Judean sojourn. Timber, however, was in short supply, and it was a long, demanding haul to obtain cedar from the Lebanon range (1.8). Haggai was impatient at such reluctance, and seems by the passion of his persuasion to have initiated a new round of Temple-building.

Still he is not satisfied. If any man still lived who could remember the earlier building he must have been a veteran indeed (2.3), but Haggai had a vision in his mind and he left the rulers and his people no rest until they caught the flash of its glory. For the new Temple, in his view, could be the one which the Messiah might see. Perhaps there was a strain of weakness in Zerubbabel, perhaps diplomatically he sought not to stir opposition (Ezra 5.4). They needed Haggai with his future look (2.9), with his exhortation to consider motives (1.5, 7) and look at the heart's faults and hesitations. Perhaps they grew old and needed youth, and, too weary, needed the salutary dash of younger energy. We would gladly know more of Haggai. What we know of him is like a refreshing breeze.

32 : Zechariah the Prophet

Zechariah 3 and 4

Along with Haggai, Zechariah must have come to Jerusalem as a child, together with Zerubbabel's pioneers. How long he prophesied it is impossible to say, but a hint of long life and two separate periods of ministry are indicated by the difference of tone between the first eight chapters and the last six.

The difference has given rise to theories of dual authorship when the perfectly natural explanation may simply be that we have in the prophet's book utterances of his young manhood and of his old age. The first eight chapters emphasize Haggai's theme. Let the people work with a will to secure a glorious destiny. In ch. 2 Zechariah has an Isaian vision of a Jerusalem which not only serves its restored people, but forms a city for the world. Here is ardent youth, dreaming its dreams and laying hold of God. Man does not stand alone. All the synthetic power of the human arm is nothing beside the enablement of God. In this faith, Zechariah puts a word of faith into the language of the Bible (4.6).

Suppose those visions and these utterances are to be dated between 520 and 518 B.C. Then consider world events. The Ionian Greek communities in Asia Minor, in Ephesus, Smyrna, Sardis and other Greek foundations, were a restless element in the western marches of the sprawling Persian Empire, and in 500 B.C a great revolt of the Ionian cities took place. Athens, just emerging to a foremost place in Greek leadership, intervened, and it was an Athenian expeditionary force which burnt Sardis in 499 B.C. Darius swore revenge, and it was his expedition of 490 B.C. which was broken by the Athenians at Marathon. Then in 480 B.C. the great expedition of Xerxes marched to its disaster at Salamis (Study No. 3).

Zechariah, now almost seventy years old, might have watched these events with absorbing interest. He mentions Greece in 9.13. He might have looked with wondering at the new movement of history. Indeed, he was witnessing the beginning of the historical process which brought Alexander to the East five or six generations later, broke down the partition between East and West, and made a Greek New Testament possible and inevitable . . .

Zechariah, in person, eludes us, but here is a picture of a man's activity for God in the spring and autumn of his life, a visionary who saw the need of the day for witness and activity, and who saw vast mysterious horizons widen as his sun went down.

33 : Ezra the Scribe

Ezra 7

Some sixty years had passed since the events of the last chapter. It is simply 'after these things' that the events of Ezra's remarkable ministry took place. Some of the personalities of this period, as we have seen, are difficult to know. They are names, men hidden in their message, or passed over by the hasty chronicler; passing shadows on the stage.

Not so Ezra. It may be assumed that he was in some sort

of official position in the Persian state organization. Daniel is an example of the high office an alien could occupy in that system, and Ezra may have been a commissioner for Jewish affairs in an empire accustomed to the government of subject peoples. Nehemiah's appointment was a further illustration. To read the letter of commission given by Artaxerxes to Ezra is to gain some insight into his standing with the Shah. The document was fairly obviously prepared and written by Ezra himself, and presented to the monarch for scrutiny and signature. The whole situation presupposes a man of worth and ability of no common order.

Ezra was a member of a family which had remained in Persia, but he represents a Jew of a far different order from the self-seeking Mordecai. He is clearly a man who had resisted integration. And more than that: realizing, like the writer we have imagined for Psa. 119, that the one strong bond of nationhood for Jewry was the corpus of their sacred Scriptures, Ezra made himself responsible for the promotion, the promulgation and the preservation of the Law. He was for this reason known as Ezra the Scribe. Ezra had 'set his heart' (10) to this task. The phrase implies an involvement of his whole personality, a complete recognition of the priority of the project. The anthologist of Psa. 119 was fond of the phrase 'with the whole heart'—could he have learned it of Ezra?

Note the two final verses of the chapter with the beautiful prayer and the final testimony. Strength, as Zechariah pointed out, comes not from man's devising, but from the enablement of God's Spirit. This was the source from which Ezra, faced with a daunting responsibility, drew the calm and poise which gave him courage. It is a blessed experience to feel the touch of 'the hand of the Lord'. Ezra was fond of the phrase (7.9; 8.18, 22).

34 : Ezra's Courage

Ezra 8

Verse 22 is one of the great verses of Scripture. Note the engaging frankness of Ezra. He valued his testimony, and had spoken bravely of his God before the Persian king. Now came the test. Hundreds of miles of bandit-ridden desert lay between the royal capital and far Jerusalem. The caravan was immensely rich with the treasures it carried. It was heavily encumbered with goods and non-combatants. Ezra was 'ashamed' to ask for an escort of armed men.

Courage is not bravado. It consists, not in blindly over-looking danger, but in seeing it and conquering it. True courage is cool and calm, and the bravest act when courage is challenged is to act as if courage is unruffled. Conscience is the root of all true courage, and conscience was rooted deep in Ezra. It lay at the foundation of his firm resolve. To feel no fear can be stupid. It may be irrational also. To dare the danger from which the mind shrinks is true nobility and the test of true worth.

And of true faith . . . There was no presuming upon God in Ezra's faith. Fasting in the ancient Jewish worship was a demonstration of earnestness and purpose. Ezra and his band gave themselves to fasting and to urgent prayer, and God heard them. Dr. Walter Adeney, in his century-old commentary on this chapter, concludes with these telling words: 'In an age of rushing activity it is hard to find the hidden springs of strength in their calm retreats. The glare of publicity starts us on the wrong track by tempting us to advertise our own excellence instead of abasing ourselves before God. Yet it is as true as ever that no boasted might of man can be comparable to the divine strength which takes possession of those who completely surrender their wills to God.'

Finally, observe in Ezra's lists family names which occurred in the earlier list of those who marched with Zerubbabel. Some of those who refused to go on the first expedition, went on the second—like Bunyan's Christiana and her children, who set out at last in Pilgrim's footsteps. Example, it is always salutary to remember, can spread its shadow, both for good and ill, over much more than one generation.

35 : Ezra's Zeal

Ezra 9.1–10.17

Ezra's deep emotion and distress over the wide incidence of interracial marriage among the Jews, was no narrow-minded reaction against natural human affection and proper regard for those of another race. There was nothing more important happening in human history at this mid-fifth century than the re-establishment of the Jewish race in its old homeland. There was no greater menace to its role in the coming centuries than the undermining and dilution of its separate witness to God.

Balaam had once taught the foes of Israel that the surest way to break their national strength was to dilute their stock with pagan inter-marriage. Ezra knew his history. He knew the lurking peril which the sex-ridden religions of Canaan held for the people (9.11). Hence his great concern over the developing menace. True, such attitudes can lead to narrow nationalism and corrupting doctrines of racial pride, but in Ezra's hands there was no intention of arrogance. He was simply urgent to keep the revived nation untainted by those influences which had brought spiritual ruin in the past.

Whether it was God's will that the harsh proposal of Shecaniah should be followed, and the alien wives and their children also should be put away, cannot be known. Ezra seems to have assented, and the act was certainly contrary to that prescribed for such mixed marriages in Corinth by Paul five centuries later (1 Cor. 7.12–16). It is sometimes the way of the reformer to drive his zeal too hard. Nor, in the brevity of the chronicler's narrative, and the chronicler seems to have concluded the book, is provision for the proper maintenance of wives and families thus put away, recorded. It is possible that material help and settlement mitigated the apparent inhumanity of the decree of banishment.

There is mention, too, of a time of cold and rain calculated to depress and daunt the spirit of the people. It is a sad sight on which the book closes, and Ezra the Scribe moves out of the page of history. He was a great and good man. Was he also a disappointed man? And did he, in the stress of his zeal, drive a correct policy beyond the frontiers of mercy? Said Addison once: 'Whether zeal or moderation be the point we aim at, let us keep fire out of the one, and frost out of the other.'

Questions and themes for study and discussion on Studies 29–35

1. Is it ever possible to see the hand of God at work in contemporary history? What of our personal lives? Is it only in retrospect that we see God's guiding hand?

2. Is it ever pleasant to stand alone?

3. Was the rebuilding of the Temple in Jerusalem significant?

4. What does Zech. 4.6 mean? What is the place of human toil in God's work?

5. What is meant by the phrase 'the hand of God'? Consult a concordance.

6. Define courage.

7. 'All true zeal for God is a zeal also for love, mercy and goodness.' (Robert E. Thompson, the American economist).

THE PERSON OF CHRIST

His Character

36 : 'He Suffered being Tempted'

Luke 4.1–15

The story of our Lord's temptation is best understood in the context of His purpose in coming into the world to be our Saviour. He is presented in the Gospel record as the second Adam, and it is this fact that gives significance to the temptations He endured, for they follow the general pattern of the temptations that came to the first Adam in the Garden of Eden. Adam and Eve were tempted to eat unlawfully (Gen. 3.1, 5); so was Christ (3). Adam and Eve were promised godlike power: 'You will be like God, knowing good and evil' (Gen. 3.5); so was Christ: 'If you, then, will worship me, it shall all be yours' (7). Adam and Eve were tempted in relation to God's word, through Satan's lying assurance, 'You will not die'; so was Christ, through the subtle misapplication of the promise of God, 'He will give His angels charge of you'. The decisive difference between the two encounters is that whereas Adam and Eve fell, Christ stood firm and unmovable. Viewed in this light, Christ's temptation represents the beginning of the counter-offensive against the kingdom of darkness that was to lead to final victory in the triumph of the cross.

It is the obedience of Christ to the will of God, and His holy determination to live in submission to His word that invests His character with incalculable worth and makes His life of such infinite value when offered in atonement for the sins of the world. In the Old Testament economy, the sacrificial lamb had to be without blemish and without spot. Christ is the truth of all the sacrifices, and He offered Himself without blemish to God for our sins.

Luke tells us that Jesus was 'full of the Holy Spirit' as He came to the wilderness from His baptism; but after His encounter with Satan, He returned to Galilee 'in the power of the Spirit'. The difference in phraseology is significant. As G. Campbell Morgan puts it, 'Fullness of the Spirit becomes the power of the Spirit through processes of testing. . . . The power of the Spirit is never realized save through some wilderness of personal conflict with the foe. From such experience, entered upon in the fullness of the Spirit, men go out either broken and incapable of service, or with the tread and force of conscious power.'

37 : The Challenge of Discipleship

Mark 10.17–22, 35–45

The story of Christ and the rich young ruler teaches us many lessons about the nature of discipleship. First, to his question about eternal life, Jesus' reply 'Why do you call me good?' has a deeper significance than is at first apparent. Rightly understood it is an assertion of His Deity. In effect He was saying, 'Do you realize that it is God the Son you are speaking to? Either I am God, or I am not good, for only God is good.' If only he had seen that it was God, the Fount of life, who was speaking to him! '*I* am eternal life, man, can't you see? Follow *Me*—that is the answer to your need.' Such was the challenge that met the ruler. But he was blind to the implications of the encounter, and when Jesus uncovered the secret idol in his life, he was shattered by the inexorable demand made upon him, in a way he would not have been if he had recognized his divine Challenger to be the Source and Giver of life itself. So, having come to the very gates of heaven, he went away sorrowful. And Jesus let him go. He is not prepared to lower the price of discipleship. With Him it must be all or nothing. The 'halfway house' has no place in His scheme of things.

The radical nature of discipleship thus underlined is further emphasized in vs. 35–45, as indeed is the true nature of goodness. When Jesus summoned the ruler to a discipleship with a cross at its heart, He was calling him to adopt His own pattern of life. 'Goodness', for Jesus, meant a life of service and sacrificial giving; it meant drinking a cup, and being baptized with a baptism, of suffering (38). The disciples were then as far out in their thinking about true goodness as the young ruler was, as the request made by James and John in vs. 35–37 shows, but our Lord's insistence on the principle of 'dying to live' (42–44) was ultimately to bear fruit in their lives, as we see in Acts. It is one of the hardest lessons in spiritual life to learn that in a fallen world real goodness can be expressed only in terms of suffering love.

Our subject is the Person of Christ. This study demonstrates that discipleship means commitment to Christ and takes His own character and sacrificial style of life as its pattern. So the Christian disciple needs to 'Consider Him!'

38 : The Supremacy of Love

1 Corinthians 13

The context of this wonderful chapter is Paul's discussion of the gifts of the Spirit which, he says, are distributed among the members of the Church, and by definition are not, and cannot be, the portion of all alike. By contrast, he now speaks of something within the reach of the humblest and most ordinary believer. The central reality in Christian experience is not the exercise of spiritual gifts, but the practice of Christian love.

The chapter divides naturally into three sections. In the first (1–3), love is contrasted with other religious actions and attitudes, and Paul takes up the spiritual gifts mentioned in the previous chapter—tongues, prophecy, discernment, knowledge, faith, benevolence ('helps', AV)—and indicates that these may flourish in believers' lives without love. When they do, life is empty; and by themselves they are not necessarily an evidence of a right relationship with God.

In the second section (4–7), love—this quality whose

absence is so deadly and fatal to the Christian life—is described in both positive and negative terms. What love is, is shown by what love does. Actions speak louder than words. The personification of love that Paul makes in these verses is significant, and it is not difficult for us to see that he is thinking of Jesus. It is for this reason we have included this chapter in this series of studies. Jesus Christ is the embodiment of love, and these qualities are fulfilled supremely and only in Him. And when He lives in our hearts by His Spirit, it is the loving Jesus that should be revealed in our actions. Love is an outgoing quality, self-forgetful and self-effacing, far removed from the self-regard and self-expression that sometimes characterize the exercise of spiritual gifts.

In the final section (8–13) love is represented as enduring and victorious, in contrast to even the best of gifts. These latter are all at best but partial revelations of the God who is love. Their place is therefore both limited and temporary. Love alone points to perfection and totality; and compared with this, other things are left behind like the ways and achievements of childhood. Paul is suggesting that the Corinthians' preoccupation with spiritual gifts rather than love is a sign of childishness and immaturity. To see that love is the supreme need, and to practise it, is to have attained true manhood and womanhood in Christ. Moreover, the character of Christ enables us to give content and definition to the word 'love' in a day when it desperately needs such definition.

39 : The Example of Christ

1 Peter 2.18–25

Peter's theme from 2.13—3.7 is submission; believers are to submit to secular power (2.13–17); servants to masters (2.18–21a); wives to husbands (3.1–7). Here he pauses to consider the example in submission that Christ has set His people. Submission is not optional for the believer, it is a calling (21a), and the basis of this calling is that Christ also suffered for us, leaving us an example that we should follow in His steps. Two things can be said about Christ's example of submission.

The first is that His submission was well pleasing to God. This is implied in v. 20, and is also evident in the fact that in His submission Christ was fulfilling the role of God's suffering Servant in the Old Testament prophecies of the Messiah. It was appointed for Him by God. The second is that His acts and attitudes of submission were redemptive. They had an end in view. He was crucified in weakness, and the weakness of God proved stronger than men, and powerfully effected salvation. This has significant application to those who follow His example, as we shall see. It is important first, however, to note that in describing our Lord's life and ministry in vs. 22 f., Peter quotes extensively from Isa. 53, a prophecy which pre-eminently unfolds the mystery of His atoning sufferings. We could hardly find a more striking evidence that the New Testament writers invariably linked Christ's life and death as belonging together in the atoning work He accomplished for our salvation. His submission in life and His submission in death cannot ultimately be separated.

His submission was redemptive; and about the worth and effect of that redemption two things are said: the first is that the death of Christ introduces a death into our experience which slays our 'old man' and imparts new life. This is healing indeed (24)! The second is that it brings us back to the Shepherd and Guardian of our souls (25), that is, we are brought back into fellowship with God, and into our true destiny.

Finally, if His submission was redemptive in its effects, and suffering is part of our calling because it was first part of His, then, although the cross stands alone as God's finished work for the salvation of men, our suffering submission and love must in some way be redemptive too. It will 'reflect', even 're-enact', His in the world, and so be a means of blessing to others. See 2 Cor. 4.10 ff.

40 : Our Great High Priest

Hebrews 4.14–5.10

The thought in this passage follows directly on that in Heb.
2.1–18, which unfolds the nature of Christ's priestly work,
Here it is the character of our great high priest that is
presented as the source and inspiration of steadfast living for
the believer (4.14, 16). It is the gentleness, understanding,
compassion and sympathy of Christ that the writer underlines
in His high-priestly character, and we can be sure of these
qualities in Him, because He has stood in with us in all our
need and tasted the suffering that is the common lot of men
(2.18; 4.15; 5.8 f.). The words 'deal gently' in 5.2 ('have compassion', AV) translate a verb which almost suggests 'to stand
in the middle of the human situation'. This means not only
that a true high priest gets alongside men in their needs and
is one with them in all their cares and anxieties, but also that
he is able to 'strike a happy mean' in his dealing with their
sins, that is, he is neither too hard, nor too lenient, in his
treatment of offenders. Neither the critical and censorious nor
the soft and sentimental can help us; our need is for one who
will not spare us and may whip us soundly, but whose heart
will be full of tenderness towards us. Christ fulfils perfectly
this 'happy mean', and those most Christlike in His service
approximate most closely to His example.

Referring in 5.7–10 to our Lord's fellow-feeling with us,
the writer turns our thoughts to the agony of Gethsemane, as
if to say 'This is how human He is'. But in what sense can it
be said that He 'was heard for His godly fear'? This cannot
refer to His prayer, 'Let this cup pass from me', for He drank
that cup. It seems to speak rather of His (unrecorded) cries
for strength to enable Him to walk the appointed way of the
cross. This is the prayer that was heard (Luke 22.43). In v. 8,
the phrase 'He learned obedience' does not mean that Jesus
learned to obey through His suffering, but rather that He
learned what obedience to the Father's will costs. It was thus
that He was made perfect (v. 9), in the sense of being brought
into His full destiny—'into His own'—as the Redeemer of
God's people and author of eternal salvation.

Questions and themes for study and discussion on Studies 36–40

1. What light do the writer's words in Heb. **2**.18 and **4**.15 shed on the Temptation story in Luke **4**?

2. Before Calvary the disciples shrank from the 'cross' principle: after Pentecost they gloried in it. What changed their attitude?

3. In 1 Cor. **13** Paul's picture of the life of love is based on the character of Christ. What does this fact teach us about the nature of the Christian life?

4. How far does Peter's teaching in 1 Pet. **2**.11–18 reflect our Lord's in Mark **10**.35–45?

5. How does Christ fulfil His high priestly role according to the writer of the Hebrews?

CHARACTER STUDIES

41 : The Cupbearer

Nehemiah 1; Matthew 6.8–13

Nehemiah was a trusted senior servant of Artaxerxes. Hanani, from whom he heard of the lamentable state of Jerusalem, was his brother (7.2). It was some thirteen years since Ezra's mission to the city, and local troubles, undisclosed in the record, had sabotaged much of the work of restoration. The ruin described could not date back to the violence of Jeremiah's day. It was local violence, of the sort which haunts the background of this book, which had so triumphed over the work of the brave band who sought to re-establish the state of Judah.

Nehemiah was a man of prayer. His grief drove him to his knees. He addresses 'the God of heaven', a Persian rather than a Hebrew form of address. It was a favourite expression of his (2.4, 20). But then he turns for general confession and supplication to the words of Deuteronomy, which were woven with the whole texture of his thought. Catch the spirit of the man in the words of his prayer. He might, in far Susa, conscious of the zeal and sincerity with which he pursued his Jewish faith, have turned from the thought of Jerusalem's woes, with timely texts to prove that all such suffering was judgement on the sins of those who had failed to make the work of restoration good.

Nehemiah adopted no such pious pose. He identified himself with his perplexed and harassed people. If judgement lay upon their sins, it was the sin of all, for all had sinned and 'come short of the glory of God'. How true it is that, in any service where the English Prayer Book is used, it is the words of the General Confession which unite all present in a common bond before God. It was a trait of folly to which Shakespeare made allusion when he coined his phrase, 'one touch of nature makes the whole world kin' (*Troilus and Cressida*, Act 3, Scene 3).

It is interesting to set Nehemiah's moving prayer side by side with the Lord's Prayer. It begins with the exaltation of God, it proceeds to confession, and only then passes in significant order to human need. Nehemiah prepared himself for confrontation with man, realizing his weakness, and resting entirely on enabling grace. It is a model we might well follow in our own prayers—to commit the significant event to God's guiding hand, to prepare our hearts before Him, to clear all impediments from the path of an answer, and to keep our clamant requests until they can assume the right perspective of worship and contrition.

42 : Royal Governor

Nehemiah 2

As he prayed before God, the Shah had been only 'this man' (1.11), but in the formidable presence of the ruler of the greatest empire in the world, Nehemiah was terrified (2.2). He nevertheless told the truth, although the devastation of Jerusalem might have been occasioned by the careless decree which misrepresentation had secured from the king ten years before (Ezra 4.11–23). Note Ezra 4.21, for the saving clause was now invoked.

All seemed well, and Nehemiah received a direct request. He shot a speedy prayer to God (4). It was four months since Nehemiah had first given himself to supplication on this theme. Now was the decisive moment. A man who can thus find God, and pray aright in a flash of time, is a man who has learned well where God may be found. The practice of ejaculatory or wordless prayer is one which should be cultivated. How often are we conscious only of a sense of desperate need, without being able to put words and sentences to the intercession! 'We do not know how to pray worthily as sons of God, but His Spirit within us is actually praying for us in those agonizing longings which never find words' (Rom. **8**.26, Phillips).

Nehemiah, curiously, mentions the queen. Perhaps she had a kindly part in the granting of Nehemiah's large request, and he thus acknowledges her beneficence. 'The good hand of my God was upon me,' he says (8), repeating, like a good disciple, Ezra's phrase (Ezra **7**.28). He set off in royal state, with a military escort (9), unlike Ezra's slow caravan. He came to Jerusalem, and, like the trained courtier that he was, said nothing to those in authority. Sanballat (10) no doubt had his spies in the city, and in the Persian Court a man learned to be wary. Nehemiah needed to know whom he could trust, and as yet he was not sure of many (16).

He was a practical man, nonetheless, and needed a clear idea of the task before him. Hence the night ride round the ruined walls. It must have been a brightly moonlit night, and the tumble of fallen masonry in the white light, and the dark shadows, must have been terrible to see. Only when in full possession of the facts did Nehemiah choose the moment, and tell the city authorities of the power that lay in his hands. Sanballat, the satrap of rival Samaria, was annoyed.

43 : Sanballat Annoyed

Nehemiah 4

Many have been the services of Egypt's sun and its rainless climate. Papyri, filled with records of the past, can lie unspoiled for ever in the dry sand and sunbaked ruins, and archaeologists have recovered them in tens of thousands. Among the most interesting papyrus records recovered are the Aramaic scrolls of Elephantine.

In the days of Persian supremacy over Palestine and Egypt a band of Jewish mercenaries in the Shah's pay garrisoned the south of Egypt at Elephantine, where the great new dam now holds the Nile. They developed a communal life, lived together with their families in a little frontier village, elected a priesthood, and built a temple, where, mixed with crude superstition, and debased by polytheistic ideas, a semblance of the worship of God was maintained. Preserved in the ruins of the high priest's house are records of sacrifices and contributions, and formulae of oath and contract, which show how the isolated community had lost much of the pure worship of Jerusalem. Strained relations with the Egyptian neighbours, due probably to the Jewish practice of animal sacrifice, led to a riot and the destruction of the temple, and some of the papyri contain the correspondence of the priest with the government at Susa in an attempt to secure permission to rebuild. The Jews knew that the royal policy was to favour the Jewish religion, for Nehemiah had already returned; but red tape was plentiful, and bribery and graft were the order of the day. The Jews of Elephantine may have trusted God, but they also, like the wary Nehemiah, believed in 'keeping their powder dry', and the letters show that they left no influential string unpulled. One man, who apparently had the ear of the chiefs in Susa, was one Sinuballit, Governor of Samaria—evidently Sanballat of Nehemiah, and now a very old man. The priest addresses two or three letters to him craving for support. He piously promises that, when the temple is rebuilt, Sinuballit shall be the subject of prayer three times a day, and, much more to the point, he adds: 'The bearer has full instructions regarding the money.'

We thus know why Sanballat hated the neighbouring Governor of Jerusalem. He could not now openly attack, or the king would have speedily removed him. A new decree had armed Nehemiah. He could, however, pin-prick and intrigue, and did so, because he was used to subservience from neighbours, flattering letters and bearers with 'full instructions regarding the money'. Nehemiah was not the sort of man to buy Sanballat's friendship, and Sanballat was annoyed. Archaeology has thrown a vivid gleam of light.

44 : Nehemiah at Work

Nehemiah 5

Chapters 4 and 5 form something of a parable. Building God's walls in this world has always been a task like this. There is always opposition to the work of God. Its commonest form is ridicule (4.1–3) which ranges from the polished sneer of the intellectual to the crude joke of the ignorant. We cannot invoke evil upon such opposition as the beleagured Jews were able to do (4.4, 5). (Read again the remarks on commination in Study No. 16.) We can, however, restore the spirit by prayer. Ridicule hurts, and we should not be human if we were not conscious of its impact.

Besides, there is a task to be done. There is no time to shrink into immobility before petty criticism. Nehemiah's people were filled with a will to work (4.6). The Church needs such folk, but it was the brave example of the leader which set them at their task.

Secondly came opposition by anger, the base resource of those whose ridicule is scorned. There was conspiracy (4.8) from Samaria in the north, Ammon in the east and Ashdod in the south-west. Nevertheless the builders prayed (4.9). Not, however, without discouragement. The sheer daunting mass of the rubbish (4.10) overwhelmed the ancient builders of the new Jerusalem, as it is likely, in a different sense, to discourage the builders of a New Jerusalem today!

Observe Nehemiah's remedy. He called to courage, and to the source of all courage, the active consciousness of the presence and the benediction of the Lord (4.14). He had practised this, found it to operate with blessing in his own life, and passed on to others the secret he had discovered.

With one hand on their swords (4.17) the builders toiled, ready to spring to arms, like the Boston minutemen of two centuries ago, at the clear call (4.18). Trust in the Lord does not preclude proper precautions and sensible care (4.22).

But neither ridicule, nor anger, nor violence is so hard to endure for a leader who bears the burden of a people as sabotage from within (5.8 f.). Note the good man's plea (5.11) for those who weakened the common effort by their inconsistency, to set matters right with God and man, and to dedicate themselves to the task . . . Nehemiah is recognizable to all who have sought with sacrifice and toil to 'build God's walls'.

45 : Nehemiah Wins

Nehemiah 6

Open opposition and the contemptible measures of hate and jealousy had failed to check the building of the walls. Nehemiah had fulfilled the role of a true leader of men—he had infused a sense of purpose into a disappointed and demoralized multitude. He had made them see that the stones which they built into the walls were more than stones, for they were symbols of renascent nationhood. It is the secret of good leadership to infuse meaning into action.

Watchfulness and alertness had won the day over the evil which had mobilized against the small band of Jews. Hence a change from threat of force to fraud, an open confession of defeat. The plot was too obvious. It was an attempt to kidnap the leader. It is not always wise to parley with the opposition. When orders are clear there can be no reason for any process of modification, and Nehemiah had his orders both from God and man.

Sanballat and his petty allies were no match for the courtier trained in the royal court. Failing in the first attempt, the Jews' foes tried threat of slander. Despotic governments are suspicious of separatist movements and personality cults. It was the sort of threat which broke Pontius Pilate. Nehemiah's conscience was clear, and he allowed no such blackmail to undermine his efforts.

The next movement of treachery came nearer to success. The man Shemaiah was a hired spy of Sanballat and Tobiah. His approach was more perilous and more subtle. He magnified the peril of assassination and counselled flight into the walled and defensible precincts of the temple. The retreat would have been a disastrous blow against the morale of the nervous population. Everything depended on the visible presence of the bold leader on the city walls. There is a self-respect which is not of pride but of faith and confidence. Nehemiah had it, and put another immortal word into Scripture (11). With this word we leave him. His story fused with Ezra's in the closing chapters of the book. His first battle for the restoration was won and it was won by faith and strength of character.

46 : The Messenger

Malachi 1 and 2

Among Nehemiah's helpers in the lax conditions which followed the completion of the major fortifications of Jerusalem was Malachi. This little book, which contains some of the most quoted passages in the Old Testament, links with the closing chapter of Nehemiah. The word Malachi means 'my messenger', and it is possible that it is not a proper name at all, but a title, under which an anonymous servant of God hides his identity.

His personality is by no means concealed. The small book is a revealing record of a ministry. It follows dialogue form and may indicate such activity as Socrates carried on in Athens just before this very date, and Paul too when, in imitation of Socratic method, he discussed the faith 'in the market-place daily with them that met him' (Acts 17.17).

'The messenger' points vigorously to the nation's coldness, questioning of God's love, unfaithfulness, and social sin. 'The market-place', or 'the man in the street' is made to answer, protesting innocence, expressing popular scepticism, and questioning the lofty standards set before them. The nation was burdened with ungrateful critics of God's providence, by unfaithful priests, by a loss of the sense of God's holiness, by lip-worship and social sin. In a sort of wide-eyed innocence, shot through with insincerity, the people at large professed inability to see how they fell short of God's claims on their lives (1.7).

Malachi takes them up point by point in strong plain prose, in that firm direct style which marked the post-exilic writers. It is a curious development. In Zephaniah prophetic literature passes into the poetry of apocalypse, of the sort which was to close the New Testament. In Habakkuk we saw the emergence of philosophic wisdom, and in Malachi we see the coming of ordered argument which was known among the Greeks, and which was to form the style of Paul, in the letter to the Roman church.

God's message can clothe itself in many forms, and the everlasting love of God, His fatherhood and holiness, emerge from the pages of Malachi as visibly as they do in Isaiah and Jeremiah. We observe, too, a growing awareness of a non-

Jewish world. Among the heathen, said Malachi, God was at times held in higher honour than among the Jews (1.11). It was the first note of a chord to be struck by Paul. Malachi not only foresaw the coming of Christ, he saw the beginning of the road to a global gospel. True, Isaiah had known some such faith, but it was the Exile which promoted it.

47 : The Remnant

Malachi 3 and 4

Sometimes in these studies we have found it profitable to look at character in the mass and in the abstract. We looked at the sad exiles, their harps on the Euphrates willow-trees, and now we must turn again, in the last chapters of the Old Testament, to the Remnant, the 'seven thousand' of Elijah's day, who did not 'bow the knee to Baal', the 'happy few' who again and again have saved a nation.

Discouragement is infectious, and a disillusioned multitude, talking like those whom Malachi quotes in 3.14, 15, can spread the contagion of their collapsed morale. It is familiar enough talk: 'It is useless to serve God. What gain is it to do His bidding and to walk in penitent garb before the Lord of Hosts? It is the worldly, we find, who are well-off; evildoers prosper. They dare God, and nothing happens to them' (mostly Moffatt).

Such words daunt the timid. In anxious times, under physical stress, in days of danger and adversity, it is easy for the lonely person, or the small harassed group, to feel beaten, and to be silenced by the loud voices of the renegade, the sceptical or the disloyal. Circumstances seem sometimes chillingly to support the faithless, and his loud unbelief.

The remedy is to close the ranks. Perspective is thereby gained and faith and wisdom beneficently pooled. 'What profit is it that we have kept His ordinances?' None, assuredly, if profit is measured by the scales and standards of evil. It is profit beyond measure if we prize our soul's salvation, our fellowship with Christ, and all that our religion means. So those who feared God more than they feared man and the menace of the world around them, came together, and God made a roll of remembrance of those who thought on His name.

A 'name' was a word of wide significance in ancient thought. It implied all that a person was; '. . . who received him, who believed in his name' (John 1.12) simply means, 'those who accepted Him for what He was'. To 'think on His name' means to fix the mind upon what God is, and that is the remedy for shaken confidence and fear. So did Malachi's Remnant, and the chapter ends with two beautiful words about them—they are God's jewels, God's beloved children (3.17). And their stand will in the coming day be vindicated (3.18)—and in the closing verses the book reaches out across four hundred years to the coming of the Lord.

Questions and themes for study and discussion on Studies 41–47

1. The use of the Lord's Prayer in private devotions.
2. Modern Sanballats and our 'building of the walls'.
3. Sabotage within in the building of the Church.
4. Prayer as a resource in mental persecution.
5. Self-confidence, good and bad.
6. Easy-going religion—is it stable, worthy, acceptable?
7. Disillusionment, disloyalty and the Remnant today.

THE PERSON OF CHRIST

His Exaltation (1)

48 : The Shepherd-King

John 2.13–22; 10.14–21

The common factor in these two passages is our Lord's reference to His dying and rising again, and they present Him in two different, though complementary, aspects. In the Temple-cleansing incident His strength and power are revealed, while in the second it is His tenderness as the Good Shepherd that predominates. Both are significant in relation to the death He died. On the one hand, in acting with authority in the Temple at the outset of His ministry He was inaugurating His work by a claim to be the King of Israel and Lord of the Temple. It was a deliberate assumption of the role of Messiah, in terms of the prophecy in Mal. 3.1 ff. And when the Jews asked Him for a sign to justify His actions, Jesus announced that His death and resurrection would authenticate His every claim and action. To speak of His death in this way was to make it plain that it was not something that happened to Him—as tragedy can happen to men—but something that He accomplished and in which He held the initiative. This is made very clear in 10.18 where He speaks of laying down His life of His own accord and taking it again. It is the voluntary nature of His dying that makes His death of unique significance and gives it its infinite worth as an act of atonement and redemption. He is the one man in all the universe on whom death had no claim as of right; that He chose freely to enter death for our sakes makes it a demonstration—and a release—of kingly power for our salvation. He did not simply suffer death, He entered it as a conqueror.

On the other hand, His claim to be the Good Shepherd (**10**.14) implies that the power in His death is the power of suffering love. The word 'good' in the Greek literally means 'beautiful', and it is the attractiveness of the goodness that is emphasized. 'I, when I am lifted up from the earth,' said Jesus, 'will draw all men to myself' (John **12**.32). There is something irresistibly attractive about the dying Saviour. In a way we can never fully understand, when Christ crucified is proclaimed, He draws men to Himself, and this is how they heed His voice (**10**.16).

49 : Weighed—and Found Wanting

Mark 12.1–12; Acts 4.5–12

The connecting link between these two passages is not only the quotation that both use from Psa. **118** about the stone the builders rejected, but also the theme of the rejection of the gospel. The parable of the vineyard sums up the whole history of the Jews. The vineyard represents the Kingdom of God. To the Jews, here represented by the husbandmen, was given the privilege of bringing in the Kingdom. But all along they failed, and their failure ultimately involved the forfeiture of all their privileges and advantages, and the transfer of them to others. The whole of Old Testament history is therefore covered by the parable. The servants in the parable represent the prophets from Samuel to John; one and all, their ministry was rejected. Jesus, then, simply rehearses the facts of history before His hearers, and in the latter part of the parable reveals what is about to happen—a dramatic situation and a devastating experience for His hearers who perceived that He was describing them. Most wonderful of all, however—and this is the force of the quotation from Psa. **118**—God has so manifested His sovereignty as to accomplish from this rejection and rebellion of His people, and their dastardly hatred of His Son, a glorious redemption for the whole world. As Paul puts it in Rom. **11**.15, God's rejection of the Jews means the reconciliation of the world.

The full content and significance of this idea is given in Acts **4**.5–12. Here, the prophecy in the parable has become historical fact, the tenants of the vineyard have put the owner's son to death, and the vineyard is about to be given to others. The rejection now, however, is seen to be less excusable than ever, for by asking 'By what power or by what name did you do this?' they were rejecting what Peter had already said in 3.16 by way of explanation, and demanding another. But there is no other explanation than that it was in the Christ whom they had slain, and whom God had raised up, an incalculable power for good had been let loose on the world. The stone that the builders rejected had indeed become the head of the corner, and the only source of salvation for all who believe in Him.

50 : 'Seeing and Believing'

John 20.1–18

One of the important lessons in John's account of the resurrection lies in his description of how its significance dawned on the disciples who went to the tomb. The word 'see' occurs repeatedly in the passage—vs. 1, 5, 6, 8, 12, 14, but the Greek is not the same in each case. Three words are used, each with a different shade of meaning. When Mary came (1) she saw that the stone was removed; this word describes the physical act of seeing. She noticed the fact, as John also did (5) when he saw the linen cloths lying. When Peter, however, saw them, another word is used, suggesting that his attention was arrested by what he saw. It was unusual, and made him look again. This word is also used in v. 12 when Mary saw the two angels. It registered with her as something unusual. Yet another word is used in v. 8 of John's 'seeing', describing an experience, and denoting perception, knowledge, understanding, and spiritual illumination. He saw, everything became clear, and he believed. What he saw was the significance of the resurrection, for it dawned on him that the claims Jesus had made about Himself, hitherto only partly comprehended, were the simple truth. He was God manifest in the flesh, as He had said, and He had passed through death as its Victor and was now alive for evermore.

This kind of 'seeing' is also evident in the encounter Mary had with the risen Lord in the garden. Mary did not come to faith and enter into peace through seeing the risen Lord with the eyes of the flesh; indeed, the physical act of seeing Him produced no reaction in her at all, for she did not even recognize Him. It was the inward 'seeing' which followed (16) that made the difference, a 'seeing' comparable to that of John's in v. 8. The words which follow in v. 17 confirm that the new relationship with Him was not to be the same as before, dependent on touch and sight—but on something more important, namely faith. What John expresses in v. 31 as the purpose of writing his Gospel had first of all become true of himself and his companions. They had 'seen' and believed. What do you see in this story?

51 : 'He Ascended into Heaven'

Acts 1.1–14

Two points in particular call for attention in this passage. The first concerns the significance of the forty days (3) during which Jesus showed Himself to His disciples. The reason why He did not ascend to the Father's right hand immediately after His resurrection is twofold: firstly, He had to open the disciples' understanding to the meaning of the work He had accomplished in His death and resurrection; and secondly, He gradually taught them, by appearing and disappearing among them, to realize that His presence with them did not depend on their seeing Him. They were being taught to believe He was with them, independently of anything they might see, hear, or feel. This was an indispensable prelim- inary to their reception of the Spirit (4, 8).

The second point is the ascension of Christ. Concerning this two things must be said. Its first significance is that He 'entered into heaven itself, now to appear in the presence of God on our behalf' (Heb. 9.24), to present the merits of His atoning work before the throne of God. In this He fulfils the office of the high priest in the Old Testament economy, whose function was to offer sacrifices for the people, to intercede for them, and to bless them from God. But it was also His enthronement and exaltation, His receiving of the Name that is above every name (Phil. 2.9), His coronation as the mighty Victor. The Christ whom we worship is not only our High Priest but a glorious King, to whom all power is given in heaven and in earth. We must not, however, think of Christ's ascension as something separate from the rest of the gospel, but as the triumphant culmination of the tremendous 'movement' of eternity which is the goodness of God to man. It is the incarnation, life, death, resurrection and ascension that constitute the saving work of Christ—and never one without the others. But it is the ascension as the climax of His finished work that is the basis of the ingathering of souls that was to take place. He won the right to men's allegiance by His death and resurrection, and the great capitulation was about to begin, at Pentecost.

52 : The Death of Death and the Death of Christ

Acts 2.22–36

The decisive importance of this passage is that it shows unmistakably what is the true nature of the gospel. Peter asserts that the fulfilment of Joel's prophecy (17–21) is associated with the life, death, resurrection and exaltation of Jesus—that is, that the outpouring was associated with the coming of the Messiah of the prophetic Scriptures, and that the Jesus whom he now proclaimed was that Messiah. There is no thought here of Jesus being merely a great religious leader martyred for his ideals. True, Peter presses the charge of the crucifixion on the Jews, but says that behind this lay the definite plan and foreknowledge of God. Christ's death was 'according to plan', the divine plan of redemption foretold in the prophetic Scriptures. It is this apostolic interpretation of the historical facts that constitutes the gospel. And it is interpretation according to the Scriptures—this is the point of the quotations from the Old Testament in vs. 25–28 and vs. 34 f., for they show that everything held together and was rooted in the divine revelation and purpose from the beginning.

The significance of v. 24 is considerable—death could not hold Jesus—for it indicates that we are to view the gospel as the divine counter-strategy over against the inroads death had made in the life of man. What Peter is saying is that when death spread to all men (Rom. 5.12) the living God declared that death should not have the last word in the human situation. The gospel is God's intervention for man's sake, to make war on death, and destroy it. In the fullness of time He came, incarnate as man, to do battle as man, for man, against the bitter enemy that reigned over all mankind. And He, who did not need to die, chose to die, thus making Him a deadly and invincible foe for the king of terrors, for He carried the war into the enemy's stronghold, taking death by storm and destroying it from the inside. And His resurrection is the practical proof that this was no fiction, but a glorious fact, which His exaltation and the subsequent coming of the Spirit brought home to the glad experience of the apostle band that day. This glorious triumph was accomplished for us too!

53 : The Apostolic Gospel and its Reception

Acts 13.16–43

Here is a characteristic example of apostolic preaching. As always, the emphasis is on the fulfilment of Old Testament prophecy in the life, death and resurrection of Christ. Paul begins with the law and the prophets that had just been read in the synagogue (15), and sweeps through Old Testament history, showing its inner meaning, and its fulfilment in the good news of the gospel. The faith of the fathers, he means, was faith in the promise of redemption, and what they all looked forward to has now taken place in the coming of Christ. Paul stresses the immense privilege given to his own generation to be the witnesses of His coming (26). True, those to whom He was sent neither recognized Him nor understood the prophecies concerning Him (27), and demanded His death. But God overruled this, for what they did was sovereignly used by God to accomplish salvation for mankind, fulfilling

77

the promise made to the fathers by raising Jesus from the dead (33).

The substance of this good news, and the meaning of the promise, is revealed in v. 38 as the forgiveness of sins and justification. It was to procure this that Jesus died and rose again. In v. 39, 'freed' translates the Greek word for 'justified', and Paul's reference in what follows to the law of Moses points the way to a true understanding of the Old Testament. The Jews' misunderstanding lay in supposing that justification could come by the law, whereas it is clear both from the New Testament and from a proper insight into the Old, that the law was never meant by God to be a means of salvation. Its purpose was preparatory; it was 'our custodian until Christ came, that we might be justified by faith' (Gal 3.24), fulfilling its function by convincing us of sin (Rom. 3.20) and therefore of our need of Him.

One wonders whether Paul felt it specially necessary to utter the word of warning in vs. 40 f. Perhaps he saw then what he was so often to see afterwards; restlessness and resistance on the part of the Jews, and refusal of his message. At all events, it is always proper for such a warning to be given, since it is a very critical—and may be a fatal—thing to react wrongly to the word of grace.

Questions and themes for study and discussion on Studies 48–53

1. What did Jesus refer to in the words 'My hour has not yet come' (John 2.4)?
2. The passage from Psa. 118 quoted in Mark 12.10 and Acts 4.11 is also quoted in 1 Pet. 2.7. What further insight does this third reference give?
3. How far would it be true to say that the full significance of the resurrection of Jesus dawned on the disciples only at Pentecost?
4. What is the relationship between the ascension of Jesus and the gift of the Holy Spirit?
5. How does Peter's message in Acts 2.22–36 compare with those in Acts 10.34–43 and Acts 13.17–41?
6. How far could it be said that Paul's words in Acts 13.26 ff. are the seed-plot of his later teaching in the Epistle to the Romans?

CHARACTER STUDIES

54 : The Simpleton

Proverbs 1 and 7

Proverbs is the inspired record of the distilled wisdom of the
Hebrews, their observations on society, the common world of
men, and human character. In this collection of sayings,
expressions of epigrammatic thought, and precepts based upon
them, several clear abstract pictures of typical individuals
emerge. They are worth looking at as we conclude the characters of the Old Testament, for men and women do not alter
fundamentally over the centuries and from race to race.

The simple person is seen in clearest detail in ch. 7, aimless,
drifting into gross temptation in sheer folly, indeed a prime
target for evil. A vivid warning picture is given of an almost
inevitable encounter in the career of the 'simple' young man.
Enter the designing temptress—and although the Hebrew
word-picture sets forth rather the enticement of the male
victim by the female designer, the reverse situation is as common and as deadly.

Proverbs makes no excuses for culpable simplicity. There is
a man who chooses not to learn. In the first chapter of the
book he meets, not a designing woman, but a band of violent
and lawless men. It is a vivid picture of an urban situation, a
group of delinquents out to rob, and likely to draw into their
vicious fellowship some newcomer without moral fortitude
who finds himself compromised and led into trouble almost
before he is aware of his peril (1.10–16).

Awareness of sin is the safeguard against sin (17), for even
a bird does not fall into a trap which it sees being set. The
trouble with the simple is a species of mental laziness. They
like their thinking to be uncomplicated and unrestricted by

principles and the hard rules of a moral code (22). To be upright, the writer urges, a man must think. There is an intellectual element in virtue (**14**.15 and **22**.3 strike this note). A simpleton is wayward out of ignorant rebellion (**1**.32). Proverbs has no regard for the empty-headed (**12**.11, **15**.21).

Temptation also contains an intellectual element. The victim is outwitted by the agent of sin. Man is a thinking creature and, under God, is expected to use his mental powers, to assess and to take to heart the consequences of wrongdoing, and to avoid the dangerous and the compromising situation. Solomon can be clearly seen behind many of these precepts.

55 : The Fool

Proverbs 2 and 9

The fool is worse than the simpleton. In Proverbs the fool is not a man without high gifts of intelligence, but one who has chosen folly as his way of life. He has no care for wisdom or for truth (**14**.8). He is a menace in society (**17**.12; **18**.7). He harms others (**10**.1; **13**.20; **17**.21, 25; **19**.13). He has no sense of proportion (**27**.3; **29**.9). He is impatient of all advice (**1**.7; **10**.8; **12**.15; **15**.5). Above all, he 'makes a mock of sin' (**14**.9 AV [KJV]). His kind still live. In this 'permissive' age they multiply. As though the lesson of all history were not the necessity for moral foundations in society, the fool spurns basic standards and the experience of all the ages. He is still a mortal danger, for he is noisy (**10**.8), expressing opinions on all subjects. He cannot be silenced (**11**.12). He is deliberately provocative (**18**.6), and an inveterate talker (**29**.11 AV [KJV]).

As a social document Proverbs takes us behind the crowded world of politics and religion, which dominate the forefront of the stage in the story of the Old Testament. The characters of Proverbs are the people of the farming community, the village lane, the back street of the city, as well as of the court and the Temple.

The fool and the wise dominate Proverbs, and bring the ancient world very close to us. The terse descriptions and penetrating aphorisms about both make the whole world one. Consider the Arabian proverb: 'A fool may be known by six things: anger without cause; speech without profit; change without progress; inquiry without object; putting trust in a stranger, and mistaking foes for friends.'

Hence the relevance of Proverbs in the conduct of everyday life. A brief phrase of concentrated wisdom can arm the mind with a quick and ready weapon for the sudden and unexpected encounter, and against fools it is well to be armed. 'I am always afraid of a fool,' said Hazlitt, 'one cannot be sure that he is not a knave.' And no man is so wise that he does not need some such arming against himself, for as Aristotle said, 'There is a foolish corner even in the mind of the wise man.' Men of all ages have the same inclinations over which the reason exercises small control. Wherever men are found, there are follies and the same follies, and the greatest of fools is he who imposes upon himself, imagines he knows that of which he is ignorant, and claims authority where he has no right to speak. The most certain mark of the fool, from Solomon's day to ours, is to think that he is always right.

56 : The Sluggard

Proverbs 6 and 26

The scorn for the sluggard, hinged to his bed (26.14), and making the most fantastic excuses to stay there (22.13; 26.13), is a sharp light on the native diligence of the Hebrew people. No one can nail the lazy fellow down to a fixed time. He hates a schedule. He is never punctual (6.9 f.). If it is difficult to get him to begin a project, it is equally difficult to make him continue to the end (12.27). Even his food grows cold (26.15). He avoids all inconvenience. Even a cold day will make him avoid his task of ploughing (20.4). Hence his restless discontent (13.4), his tangled affairs (15.19), and his uselessness in any employment (10.26; 18.9).

The famous passage about the ant (6. 6–8) shows that the lazy fellow is running counter to the whole course of nature.

Battle with the adverse forces of the world is part of the human lot, which is shared by the brute creation. A vital difference between the lazy and improvident man and the diligent ant is that the ant needs no prodding (6.7), and by some inner awareness knows the needs of time and season (8). To the sluggard it is 'always afternoon.' No menace looms. Hence sudden disaster. The sharp and irremediable arrival of poverty takes him by surprise. It comes to his door like an unexpected guest, or like some villain springing, weapon in hand, out of an ambush by the roadside (6.11).

In a word, the sluggard serves as a shocking warning to the sensible. Look at **24**.30–34. The wise man looks at the weed-ridden field of the fellow who was too warm in bed to get out to the spring ploughing, and observes the lesson of the weeds and tangled growth. He knows that the sluggard is a man just as he is, but a man who has enjoyed his comforts too much and too long, has filled his weakling's mouth with empty excuses, and little by little has slid down to moral and social disaster.

Sloth, no doubt, smothers virtue, lives on deepening mental torpidity and ruins life. Life, in the word's truest sense, is the mark of the Christian, and life carries in its very meaning, the notion of alertness, the energy of the mind, swiftness of action and diligence in business. Nations die of sloth, and sluggards, the slugs of the wider garden, have brought peoples to decay. Man is a worker. If he is not that, he is nothing. Work is the condition of our being, from Eden to Paul (Gen. **3**.17 ff.; 2 Thess. **3**.11 f.). Proverbs was right. The sluggard is a figure of scorn.

57 : The Scoffer

Proverbs 21 and 22

D. Kidner, in his splendid commentary (Tyndale O.T. Commentaries), points out that the scoffer or scorner makes seventeen appearances in Proverbs, and is most commonly associated with the fool. Again, it is 'mental attitude rather than mental capacity' which classifies the man.

The scoffer, like the fool, abhors correction (**9**.7 f.; **13**.1; **15**.12). He is a peril in society, and a source of damage, but it is deeper and more sinister damage than that of the fool. He is the deliberate destroyer of good things (**21**.24; **22**.10). He is dangerous enough to lead whole communities astray (**19**.25), but good men are usually sufficiently alert to him (**24**.9). He falls under the direct judgement of God (**3**.34).

How well we know him! Ridicule, in this artificially sophisticated world, is a common weapon against the Christian, but it is 'the way the Master went'. 'They laughed Him to scorn ... and those that passed by mocked Him and said, He saved others, Himself He cannot save' (cf. Mark **15**.29–31; Luke **23**.35). Mockery is always 'the fume of little minds', and the scoffer contemptible, whether he be the crude coward who laughs at youth's desire to be upright, or the polished worldling raising the scornful eyebrow at the Christian who refuses to pay the price of joining what C. S. Lewis called 'the inner ring'.

Ridicule through all the ages has become almost a test of truth. There is pain, to be sure, in being laughed at, but the ridiculed of all the centuries are a most distinguished and honourable company. Therefore let it cause no shock, no disappointment, no disillusionment if a clear testimony brings damage to popularity, or brings rejection or loss of this worldly advantage or that.

The scoffer steps out of the pages of Proverbs, a small and familiar figure. He changes his garb with age, status and society. His face remains the same, with the lines of Satan upon it. Watch him march on, and pity him for his folly, for his cowardice, for his jealousy and for all the other acid-laden vices which eat away his mind and heart. He is at odds with himself, playing a petty part. He fears the things which he attempts to scorn. Watch him march on, for he marches to the Judgement Seat, and it will be difficult when 'the books are opened' to find extenuation or excuse for one of the lowest and most loathsome of human sins ... or, if one can, love him, as Goldsmith's good vicar did. In his church there were 'fools, who came to scoff, who stayed to pray'.

58 : The Friend

Proverbs 17 and 18

In an earlier study (Vol. 4, Study No. 39) we looked at the friendship of David and Jonathan. The picture painted by Proverbs, a line here and a line there, of the real friend, might have been taken from the story of that famous partnership.

Constancy is the prime quality of the friend, for constancy is the complement of all the other virtues. Joseph Addison had that thought in mind when he said: 'Without constancy, there is neither love, friendship nor virtue in the world.' See **17**.17 and **18**.24. Candour, Proverbs says, is another necessary quality (**27**.6), but let it be candour with love. One touch of malice, and all friendship is belied. Consider Job's friends. 'If we be honest with ourselves,' said George MacDonald, 'we shall be honest with each other.' At the same time, Paul said: 'Love covers up.' Let a balance be struck.

There are two magnificent sayings about friendship and fruitful fellowship in ch. **27** (9 RSV mg. and 17). Counsel, and the willingness and ability to give wise advice, are the marks of the good and worthy friend. To have a kindred spirit to whom to turn in perplexity and doubt is a rare privilege. And then, as iron sharpens iron, there is the rub and polishing of like with like. This situation presupposes mutual goodness. Set David and Jonathan against Rehoboam and his designing friends. 'Counsel and conversation,' said Clarendon, 'are a second education, which improve all the virtue and correct all the vice of the first, and of nature itself'.

Is it not a fact that a wise man is apt to be diffident about himself and on that account is willing to listen to counsel? The foolish man is full of himself, despises advice and amputates friendship in the same act, seeking counsel only in his fallible self.

Tact is the fourth and final mark of a friend. A friend does not outstay his welcome (**25**.17), display a repugnant heartiness at the wrong time (**27**.14), or act with unwitting cruelty (**25**.20). Tact is a fragile and delicate virtue. It comes from goodness of heart and delicacy of taste. The good friend knows the untimely and inappropriate joke (**26**.18 f.). Tact is everything. It is not a sixth sense, but is the life of all the other five.

Friendship needs guarding. Malice seeks to estrange (**16**.28). In other words there is a spiritual element which binds and seals and fructifies. We can bless God for the friend of Proverbs if he come our way.

59 : Women

Proverbs 5 and 31

The latter portion of the last chapter of Proverbs is an acrostic, which D. Kidner calls 'an alphabet of wifely excellence'. It is a separate portion in the Septuagint, adding weight to the suggestion that it is a piece by an unknown author, rather than a continuation of the words of Lemuel's mother.

It is a portrait of a lady of means with servants under her and money to invest (16. f.). She is the financial partner of her husband, with duties in the estate and in the city (11–18, 24). She is a tireless person, ready with her charity, and shrewd in her preparations for the future (15, 18, 19, 20, 21, 27). She is nonetheless a kindly, human person, not rendered hard by her business and financial preoccupations (20), a happy, loving mother, and a good wife. She owes her strength to her faith (25, 30), and her dedicated intelligence (28–31).

The portrait of the good woman is a special one. It implies a certain status in society and, as Kidner puts it: '. . . it shows the fullest flowering of domesticity, which is revealed in no petty nor restricted sphere, and its mistress as no cipher. Here is scope for formidable powers and great achievements—the latter partly in the realm of the housewife's own nurture and produce (31) and partly in her unseen contribution to her husband's good name (23).'

The portrait of the bad woman in ch. **5** is much more down to earth, and reflects Proverbs' lofty view of the sanctity of marriage and its opinion of the disrupter of such fidelity. Chapter **7** also speaks of her. The loose woman sells a parody of love. She erodes honour (**5**.9; **6**.33), liberty (**23**.27 f.), possessions (**6**.26; **29**.3), and breathes physical danger (**6**.26–35). To seek life in such a context is to flirt with death (**2**.18 f.). It is to take the smooth path to the grave.

It is refreshing to find this book of Hebrew wisdom so

clear and sharp in its understanding of the social and psychological ruin which sexual laxity contains. A nation is measured by the standards of its women. When women such as the blatant and thrusting bad women of this book are active in society, to the corruption of fools and simpletons, disaster is near.

Questions and themes for study and discussion on Studies 54–59

1. How far does intelligence enter into goodness?
2. The right attitude when men scoff at our deepest convictions.
3. The sluggard in modern society.
4. The ideal friend.
5. The ideal woman.

THE PERSON OF CHRIST

His Exaltation (2)

60 : 'According to the Scriptures'

1 Corinthians 15.1–11

This chapter is one of the most magnificent in all Scripture. Its first section (1–11) deals with the fact of the resurrection, and what follows with its implications. Paul sets his teaching in the context of the gospel message itself (1), reminding us that we are not entitled to emphasize the death of Christ to the exclusion of the resurrection, or vice versa. Both are essential. The message he delivered at Corinth was 'that Christ died for our sins . . . and that He rose again the third day according to the scriptures' (3 f.); this is what constitutes the gospel.

We are given in these verses a threefold proof of the reality of the resurrection of Christ. First, the existence of saved men and women (1 f.)—the fact of the Church—is a compelling proof of the resurrection, for here are men and women who themselves have been raised to newness of life. Note Paul's words, 'you received . . . you stand . . . you are saved'. This is what lifts the doctrine out of the realm of theory and speculation, and makes a believer certain. He knows—for it has happened to him.

Secondly, Paul substantiates the resurrection from the Scriptures (4). The resurrection of Jesus was not a hastily concocted fiction stuck on to the story by the disciples to give it a happy ending, but something integral to the strategy of God and foretold by the very Scriptures that prophesied His death (cf. Pss. **2**.7; **16**.10; **22**.22 ff.; Isa. **53**.10).

Thirdly, there is the testimony of the eyewitnesses (5–8).

The implications here are very impressive and far reaching, particularly the fact that most of the five hundred referred to in v. 6 were still alive and could have disputed Paul's assertion if it had not happened. When one thinks of the flimsy evidence on which scientists sometimes make such confident pronouncements, and how prone some are to dispute that on which the gospel is based, it becomes only too clear that their objections to the Christian message are often based on moral, rather than intellectual, grounds. Once the validity of the evidence given here is admitted—and it is far too authentically documented to be questioned—one is obliged to kneel down and own Christ Lord of all. And this is what the proud heart of man is not prepared to do.

61 : 'Christ is Risen'

1 Corinthians 15.12–28

In these verses Paul deals with the implications of the resurrection. Some in Corinth held that there was no resurrection from the dead, i.e. that resurrection, as a concept, was unthinkable. Paul here shows the logical conclusion of this Sadducean unbelief. If resurrection *per se* is unthinkable, Christ could not have risen; and if Christ is not risen, 'your faith is futile, and you are still in your sins' (17). The explanation of this categorical statement is that the resurrection of Christ was God's imprimatur on the finished work of the cross, the divine seal of approval on the worth of His atoning death. Christ died for our sins, suffering as the Just for the unjust, to bring us to God, being set forth as a propitiation, making atonement for sin—all this the Scriptures teach, and to this He bore witness when He cried 'It is finished.' But was He right, and are these statements true? How can we be sure? What proof is there that atonement *was* made? Ultimately, only God could answer these questions, and the resurrection was God's 'Yes' to them all, His proclamation to the world that the death of Christ was sufficient to procure our everlasting salvation. This is how central the resurrection of Christ is. It alone enables us to proclaim with assurance that 'Christ died for our sins.'

Next, Paul links the resurrection of men with that of Christ (22 ff). Adam and Christ are spoken of as representative figures, the heads of the old humanity and the new. When Adam sinned, all the family of men sinned and fell in him. But there is a second family, the family of God in Christ, all members of which partake of the blessings of its Head. All that Christ did was for us, and when He triumphed over sin and Satan, we became victorious in Him. Thus, those who believe in Him not only share in His risen life now, but shall do ultimately in the fullest measure (22, f.). The redeemed in Christ shall finally be gathered home, and the resurrection of Christ as first-fruits is the pledge and guarantee of the final harvest when the Church is glorified. Ultimately, all in the universe will be subdued under Him (25–28). The resurrection of Christ has incalculable, even cosmic, repercussions.

62 : Head Over All Things—For Us!

Ephesians 1.15–23

Paul now passes from his exposition of our riches in Christ (3–14) to the prayer that we might enter fully into them. It is a prayer that the Holy Spirit will make personal in us the work of Christ for us. It has three parts, corresponding to statements made in vs. 3–14, the first with v. 4, the second with v. 11, the third with v. 13.

The hope to which He has called us is the hope of glory (Col. 1.27), of our ultimate conformity to His image (Rom. 8.29; Phil. 3.21). When once the grandeur and magnitude of this reality grips us, it will become an anchor of the soul (Heb. 6.19), making us steadfast and immovable in all the storms of life. In the New Testament 'the blessed hope' is an incentive and encouragement to holiness and steadfastness of life.

The phrase 'in the saints' (18) can mean 'among the saints'. Paul would then mean it is not possible fully to know the riches of God's glorious inheritance except in fellowship. It is when we are together that that fullness dawns on us. If we take 'in the saints' literally, it refers to what God is intent on doing in us for Himself, in preparing a people for His own possession (cf. Eph. 5.27). To know what God is aiming at in our lives will not only help us understand all His dealings with us, but also enable us to co-operate gladly with Him in willing obedience and submission.

This passage owes its place in this series on Christ's person to Paul's third petition. Here (19 ff.) two points must be noted. One is that the 'power in us who believe' is the Holy Spirit, since it is the same power as was at work in Christ, who offered Himself without blemish to God through the eternal Spirit (Heb. 9.14), and was designated Son of God with power according to the Spirit of holiness by His resurrection from the dead (Rom. 1.4). The other is that the Spirit comes to us to work the same pattern in us as He did in Christ, 'repeating' in us the process of death, resurrection, and exaltation. His being made head over all things was not for Himself alone, but for us (22), and He 'makes over' that immense victory to us by His Spirit. It is for a knowledge and understanding of this that Paul prays so earnestly in these verses.

63 : Stooping to Conquer

Philippians 2.1–13

This passage contains one of the mightiest and most sublime utterances Paul ever made. It describes the mind of Christ as He became incarnate to save us. Paul's portrayal of the downward steps of Christ's humiliation is very moving. From glory to shame, from crown to curse He came, to stand with us in our woe and lift us from it by the infinite worth and power of His descent. 'In the form of God' means that constitutionally, in the essence of His being, He was God. Yet He did not count equality with God a thing to be grasped, to be hugged to Himself, but voluntarily surrendered it in the interests of the world's redemption. A contrast between the first and last Adam may lie behind Paul's thinking here. In the story of the Fall (Gen. 3) it was precisely equality with

90

God that Adam did grasp at ('you will be like God'). But Christ, who could have claimed this as of right, regarded it as something to be surrendered. Not in that way was He to attain man's submission to Him as Lord. So He emptied Himself, not divesting Himself of His Godhead or of the attributes of Deity, as some would have us believe, but pouring out His soul to death (Isa. 53.12), accepting death as obedience to the Father's will. Because of this God highly exalted Him—this is the point of 'therefore' in v. 9. The humiliation is the basis of the exaltation. The significance of this is profound and decisive: Christ's exaltation to the Father's right hand and His being given a name mean that He was raised to a place of equality with God. What He refused to grasp as His right is now freely given Him by God as the fruit of His passion and victory. The 'name' He is given is that of Yahweh, Lord. Paul is clearly quoting from Isa. 45.23 and attributing to Christ what originally belonged to Yahweh.

The summons 'work out your own salvation' (12) corresponds to 'Have this mind among yourselves' (5). When that awesome self-emptying and subsequent exaltation (6–11) touches our lives, as it does by the operation of the Spirit of God, it will produce in us the kind of spirit Paul describes in vs. 1–4, and the mind of Christ will be manifest in us.

64 : Suffering and Glory

1 Peter 1.10–21

The distinctive importance of this passage is that it relates the sufferings and subsequent glory of Christ to the Old Testament prophecies. The gospel has its roots in the Old Testament, and there is an essential unity between the Old and the New. The whole of the biblical revelation has to do with the gospel, and this fact is an indispensable key to a proper understanding of the Scriptures as 'the history of the promise'. This enables Peter to speak of the Spirit of Christ at work in the prophets (11) without any sense of incongruity. The Christian position commits us to this viewpoint, for the doctrine of the Trinity implies the *eternal* Sonship of Christ, and it is the Spirit's work to testify of Him, in whatever age (John 15.26). In the old dispensation the vision was for an appointed time; their hope was in the promise, and in the God-appointed symbols and shadows of things to come, which pointed beyond themselves (12). Hence the reference to Christ as 'a lamb without blemish or spot' (19): the sacrifices were shadows cast on the course of history by the Lamb slain from the foundation of the world. He is the truth of all the sacrifices, and the relation between the two great dispensations is that of promise to fulfilment. It was this that the Spirit revealed to the prophets.

The sufferings and glory of Christ are reflected in the two-fold strand in the Old Testament's prophetic teaching, some prophecies stressing the idea of the coming of a glorious King, others depicting the suffering Servant of God. This second idea was largely obscured and misunderstood by the Jews, hence the difficulty the disciples had with the thought that 'the Son of man must suffer' (Mark 8.31), and the apostolic insistence, later, that this was the heart of the gospel (Acts 17.3). This was the good news they preached through the Holy Spirit sent from heaven (12).

'Ransomed' (AV, 'redeemed', 18) has the force of 'set free by the payment of a price', and Peter speaks here of the great deliverance from sin's guilt and power achieved by the blood of the cross, which establishes the new covenant that ends the old dispensation and fulfils it. Christ is the Passover Lamb by which men are brought into a new relationship and fellowship with God.

65 : The Magnitude of Christ

Revelation 1.9–20

John is on Patmos, in exile for Christ's sake, but he is conscious of belonging to two worlds: he is also 'in the Spirit', and this unseen world becomes more vital and real than his visible experience of exile as the living, exalted Christ (17 f.) breaks in on his consciousness, imparting in vision a message of wonderful encouragement to hard-pressed believers in every age.

Three points in particular should be noted. The first is the assurance that no matter how severe the suffering and pressure experienced by God's people may be, the living Christ stands among them. Independent of any consciousness or sense of His presence and even in the teeth of the most realistic impressions that deny it, He is there. His Alpha and Omega (the first and last letters of the Greek alphabet) indicate that tribulation is bounded by the living Christ. He is there before it begins and after it is over. Every Patmos is encompassed by the everlasting arms.

The second point is the impression of great magnitude conveyed in the words that describe the Christ who appeared to John, eyes like a flame of fire and voice as the sound of many waters. Above all else this is the conception of Christ that the Church needs in time of trial. What John needed, surrounded as he was by the barren rocks of Patmos and the cruel jailors, with the wide sea cutting him off from fellowship with God's people, was the sight of majesty and glory, and this is what was given him in the vision of the exalted Christ in the midst of the lampstands.

Finally, something needs to be said about the nature of Christ's exaltation. It is not merely a sequel to His dying and rising again, or the culmination of His saving work. It is that; but it is more, for that saving work was a triumph over all His enemies. His exaltation is therefore His assumption of the place of power where He takes action to fulfil His plans for His Church. This is an 'official' position, which gives Him authority over all, and is what having 'the keys of Death and Hades' means. He is in sovereign control. Well might He say to John, 'Fear not'! Who could fear with such a glorious Lord standing with him?

Questions and themes for study and discussion on Studies 60–65

1. What can we learn from 1 Cor. **15**. 1–11 about the preaching of the early Church?
2. What is it about Christ's resurrection (1 Cor. **15**.12–28) that is so crucial for the very existence of the Christian faith?

3. What is the relevance of Christ's exaltation to His Church today?

4. What does Phil. 2.5–13 tell us about what God thinks of His Son's self-emptying?

5. If the gospel that centres in Christ is rooted in the Old Testament Scriptures (1 Pet. 1.10 ff.), how is it that the Jews were so blind to its truth?

6. On what grounds can we legitimately apply to ourselves the assurances that were given to John in the vision that came to him on Patmos (Rev. 1)?

CHARACTER STUDIES

66 : Righteous Job

Job 1.1–5; Psalm 37

The book of Job, with its magnificent poetry and drama, deals with the age-old problem of human pain and unmerited suffering. Its hero is a man outside the Covenant, who was not a Hebrew. Job of Uz was an Arab, and he breaks into Scripture with the suddenness of the good king of Salem, Melchisedek. Like Abraham's friend, Job shows a knowledge of God which is outside the main stream of the Old Testament revelation. The story is told by a great poet of superb dramatic power, and the characters live before us with compelling vividness.

Job was a man of wealth, and since, in his social context, wealth and prosperity suggested the favour of heaven, Job was regarded with veneration. He was the emir of his district, the judge at the city gate. Friendliness and idyllic joy marked his household, and in fine solicitude the good man watched over his family joy, and yearned for their virtue and godliness. Job's children were dear to him, and he wanted his loved ones to know the peace in God that was his.

Job feared the Most High God, and brought offerings of humility to Him. No trace of idolatry or superstition lurks in his simple and reverent faith. He makes no mention of the Hebrew Covenant, and the promises to Moses. Presumably his was a trust born of an earlier revelation, a more ancient tradition. And from such high belief flowed character as noble and as good. Four qualities distinguish him (1.1), and together they form a picture of worth and piety without flaw or blemish. Towards man, Job was upright and beyond

95

reproach, towards God Almighty, reverent, obedient, grateful and of unsullied virtue. An honoured chief, he ruled in wisdom and in righteousness, and was known by reputation to a wider circle than his own immediate tribal environment.

Job lived in a sort of dream world, in which the knowledge of God, for which the writer of Psa. 37 bids the puzzled child of God wait in patient trust, had seemed to come in automatic simplicity. All was well with Job's tranquil heart, and all was well around him. True, the faith of Psa. 37 was the faith of Job, but it had never been tested by disaster. It had appeared that all good came his way without his waiting. Naturally enough in a species of quiet innocence, Job thought that God thus gave when, in justice, mercy, love and peace, a man played his part in truth.

67 : Satan

Job 1.6–2.7; Matthew 4.1–11

The reality of a personal power of evil is taken for granted in the strange drama of this passage. The significance of the story is God's permissive will. He is never the author of evil, but for some inscrutable reason He permits it. Satan, flitting cynically through these verses, is not Dante's misshapen monster, nor Milton's royal and arrogant rebel. Goethe's Mephistopheles is nearer the truth—the corrupter who seeks to persuade that evil is good, and virtue is folly. Above all he is the Accuser, the creature ready to see a challenge in all good, a spur to malevolence in all virtue, a target in all righteousness. As such he finds daily and universal reflection in the multitude of those who are 'of their father the devil, and the lusts of their father they will do' (John 8.44). Moral evil is the basis of Satan's character (Matt. 13.19, 39). He naturally twists and perverts, lives in hate, and opposes all desire and ambition for good. The lie of Eden sets the tone. He never departs from it. Hence his Accuser's role in Job. It never ceases.

> *'I sinned. Then straightway, post haste,*
> *Satan flew*
> *Before the presence of the most high God*
> *And made a railing accusation there.*
> *He said: "This soul, this thing of clay*
> *and sod,*
> *Has sinned. 'Tis true that he has named*
> *Thy name;*
> *But I demand his death, for Thou hast said:*
> *"The soul that sinneth it shall die."*
> *Shall not*
> *Thy sentence be fulfilled? Is Justice dead?*
> *Send now this wretched sinner to his doom;*
> *What other thing can righteous ruler do?"'*

For this reason, said John (1 John 3.8), was the Son of God made manifest—to destroy the Accuser and his works. And not only Accuser but Tempter. As such Satan laid hold upon the Lord Himself, taking natural desires, normal ambitions, and seeking to bend and pervert them into processes of rebellion.

Job's prologue, then, sets certain truths down as axioms. The first is that Satan initiates evil. A personality and a plotting mind are behind sin. Surely activity lacks explanation, but in experience is real enough. The second is that God permits evil, but turns evil into good.

68 : Job's Wife

Job 2; Romans 12.9–16

Troubles common to that time and place fell belatedly on Job, but fell in fury, and to crown all came the horror of some tropical disease which befouled his body and took away all dignity and comeliness. With it, and 'most unkindest cut of all', came the broken faith of Job's wife. It cannot be said whether it was in pity or in disloyalty that she gave her afflicted husband her dreadful advice. Clearly enough, she thought that his quiet faith of earlier years had betrayed him, and that some malevolent spirit was his God, ready, in a last gush of anger, to precipitate an end which could only be glad release.

Job's answer to her is one of the fine touches of the book. 'You speak,' he quietly replied, 'like a foolish woman.' He implies by the last two words that her advice was out of character. It was not like her to utter such words of desperation. The same words had nonetheless cut deep. Both AV (KJV) and RSV use the word 'integrity' in v. 9. The Hebrew noun means rather 'innocence' or 'simplicity', and that is how Jerome rendered it in his Vulgate version. Knox, who follows Jerome's Latin, thus renders it 'innocence'. Job's faith had indeed been simple and uncomplicated. He had held the tranquil innocence and simple view of God and the world at which his wife now flings a sophisticated sneer. It is hard to be hit thus where the heart is vulnerable.

And it is as hard to be thus met with disloyalty and contempt, where loyalty and love might properly have been expected. A man can endure much at the callous hands of the hostile world, so long as home and home's guardian remains a solid refuge. With home a base on which a battered man can retire to rearm and go emboldened forth again, society can do its worst and a man can laugh and bear it unmoved. Horatius, in the Roman story, as Macaulay told it, 'saw on Palatinus the white porch of his home', and, strengthened by the sight of it and what he knew was there, turned and faced the Etruscan army, while Rome's defenders hacked down the Tiber bridge behind him.

Job 'lay in dust, life's glory dead', and now there was no one to make home the ultimate earthly refuge, with loyalty on guard there and understanding. Home was gone, for a familiar voice had turned bitter. At that moment Job's control was supremely tested. He prevailed, and no word of evil passed his lips. Hence the deep significance of the last sentence of v. 10. It was one of Job's triumphant hours.

69 : Job's Despair

Job 3

Job was horribly alone. Then came his three friends. They have gone down in history and the languages of man as worthless comforters, and people of small understanding. This is hardly fair. There was worth and reality in their friendship, helpless though they proved to be in the face of crushing calamity. They wept and took their place by Job's side, and sat for seven days in silent sympathy, struggling with their thoughts. Here, surely, was fellowship more real than some friends give. Like Ezekiel with the exiles by the Chebar canal, they 'sat where he sat', and might have lifted a little of the burden of Job's pain. It was far from being a heartless undertaking.

And yet it provoked somehow Job's outburst of tragic despair. Perhaps his agony called for words, any words, and perhaps he misconstrued their patent helplessness as lack of understanding. Or perhaps he misread the six puzzled eyes turned upon him from beneath the dusty burnous, and read disapproval, where there was only bewilderment too great to permit speech.

In the desolate horror of his disease Job was no sight for contemplation. There was shame in his physical torment. Hence his first complete loss of self-command, his vehemence and descent into unreason. Job is magnificently free from all taint of superstition, and yet, in his quite elaborate cursing of the day of his birth, he seems to succumb to some pagan notion that present and future can be swept of ill if the noisome pile of evil things can be thrust back on to some dark, infelicitous day of doom. His words seem too detailed to be a mere expression of present pain.

The closing verses speak of almost unbearable agony. Job finds no end or purpose in staying alive. 'There is energy enough,' writes R. A. Watson, 'to feel life a terror and no more—not enough for any mastery, even of stoical resolve.' Moffatt's rendering makes good sense of the closing two verses. It was the RV, followed by the RSV, which saw the advantage of the present tenses. The words become then a cry of ultimate pessimism, born of black despair. Job touches the depths. 'Whate'er I fear befalls me, and what I dread draws on me. I get no peace, I get no rest. I get no ease, only attacks of agony.'

70 : Eliphaz

Job 4 and 5

Job's outbursts of dark despair seem to have provoked
Eliphaz to speech, and to harsh judgement. Sympathy, if such
there had been while Eliphaz sat with his friend, was now
dashed with horror. Eliphaz' simple view of sin and suffering
was no doubt that which Job himself had held in the days
before his calamity. Eliphaz is a man of eloquence, of poetry
and of Oriental politeness—and of obtuseness.

In his first eleven verses Eliphaz speaks in sorrow. Job
himself, he says, has professed to know the answers. Now
he must endure them. Where, he asks, more in sorrow than
in reproach, is his trust in God of other days? Eliphaz knows
that life works on a plain, clear law—as a man sows he
inevitably reaps, and the crop of sin's sowing is disaster, sick-
ness and pain. Job must therefore humble himself and confess
his sin.

And who more than Eliphaz had the right thus to expostu-
late? He had once had a remarkable experience of spiritual
things. In some moving and unforgettable vision of the night
he had been made aware of another world, and a voice
emerged from it (17). The fact that the words were a truism,
and had often been said by humble men before a holy God,
was nothing to Eliphaz. He had been singled out for divine
instruction. A 'charisma', if the overworked term may be
used, lay now upon him, and made his utterances words of
uncommon worth.

Eliphaz has nothing new to say. He has seen before such
catastrophes as those that have lain Job low (5.1–7).
without self-criticism, analysis or comprehension. A quirk of
the mind had been laid hold of by him as a manifestation
of God's special favour, a compliment from the Most High.
The visitation of the Holy Spirit should abash, humble, and
recreate. It should not, and cannot, minister to pride.

Eliphaz has nothing new to say. He has seen before such
catastrophes as those that have lain Job low (5.1–7).
Indeed, they are the common lot of man. But cannot Job
turn to God, the great restorer (8 f.), who is plenteous in
mercy? All this is said on the assumption that, through the
long and weary nights of his calamity, Job had not been

doing exactly that. His despair was precisely because no clear answer seemed to come. He implies that Job has been a devious and crafty man (12 f.), and was reaping the visible fruit of secret sowing. He pours out obvious truths, dogmas of common knowledge, the religious sentiments of the comfortable, the untried, the prosperous. He gets nowhere near the seat and fountain of Job's pain. He knows all the answers —and knows none.

71 : Job Attacks

Job 6 and 7

Eliphaz has roused the sufferer to some resentment. Job's mind seems to be released from torpor, and, from the mood of dark hopelessness of his first speech, his strong mind springs to life. He stands obviously above Eliphaz in power of understanding and coherent utterance. True, he says, he has spoken rashly. Eliphaz hit home here. But let that fault be set side by side with the load and magnitude of his immense suffering (6.1–7). The very animals complain only when their need is not met. Man lives by more than bread, and Job starves for the food and sustenance of true understanding.

The overwhelming desire to have done with it all and find the peace of the grave sweeps over him again (8–13), and the sombre mood seems to have been stirred by the shock of his disappointment. When his friends came from so far to comfort him, Job had looked for the words of counsel or of love which faithful friends can give. He wanted nothing more. Such gifts outweigh all material bounty (22 f.), and for help in the restoration of his earthly fortunes he was in no mood to ask.

Like the thirsty caravan struggling on through the arid wilderness to the place of waters, and finding the valley dry (14–21), so had Job himself been. He saw his friends' coming as the hope of sustenance, and like the drought-stricken riverbed, they were dry of all that which his wildly thirsting soul might have drunk.

Failing this, then let them at least convincingly instruct

101

him. Let them not be hard, but let them show him wherein he had erred . . . In the next chapter Job seems to turn from his helpless friends to God. He complains of the misery of his nights and days, and then in bold, frank words expostulates with the Lord. Why should One so high and mighty be concerned to hem round with troubles the puny life of one insignificant man? Almost inverting the language of Psa. **8**, Job boldly asks why the God of all the high heavens should concern Himself with afflicting man so small, so ephemeral, so doomed. They are powerful and daring words for one so pious. Job reaches for something unknown, unrevealed. It was to come in Christ, clothed in whose righteousness man can approach the eternal throne, '. . . little children remember to live continually in him. So that if he were suddenly to reveal himself we should still know exactly where we stand, and should not have to shrink away from his presence' (1 John **2**.28, Phillips).

72 : Bildad

Job 8; 1 Corinthians 13

Bildad of Shuach now intrudes. He lacks the polish of Eliphaz. He is not perhaps as brutal as Zophar, but he is a man without pity. All the answers are in his creed. Job's children would not have died had they not earned death by their sin. He is the man who has a text for all eventualities, prefabricated solutions for all the problems and all the perplexities of life.

In fact, wisdom of old time had codified it all. Today Bildad would use the Bible as a bludgeon rather than a balm. His memorized texts, along with his own dogmatic interpretation of them, would be brought to bear upon the situation, and no other comment would be possible. H. L. Ellison aptly contrasts him with John Robinson, the good pastor of the Pilgrim Fathers: 'I charge you before God and His blessed angels that you follow me no farther than you have seen me follow Jesus Christ. If God reveals anything to you by any other instruments of His, be as ready to receive it as you were to receive any truth by my ministry, for I am verily persuaded that the Lord hath more truth yet to break forth out of His holy Word.'

Not so with Bildad. All truth was of old revealed—and to Bildad. Job sat in misery. Heavy affliction marred and wasted him. Pain and distress were the reward of sin. Therefore Job had sinned. Can the river-reed, the lush papyrus grow, unless there be water round its roots? With such smoke there is surely fire. 'The tent of the wicked will be no more' (22). It was all as simple as that. Job was judged of God.

Such purveyors of simple and orthodox solutions have their place in the affairs of men. It must be admitted that their comments are often correct, but such vindication of traditional and proverbial wisdom serves only to harden them in their preconceived patterns of thought. They betray little love, and are prone to blurt out the damaging word with no thought of pain inflicted.

Bildad has been provoked to speak by Job's protestations of innocence. He, too, shows that the relations between the participants in the dialogue are deteriorating.

73 : Bold Thinker

Job 9 and 10

Job answers wearily. He is infinitely sad. He could have foretold all the words of Bildad. Of course God is just. Of course man cannot vindicate himself before Him. But that assertion does not touch his bitter problem. God has condemned him, and he knows not why. And how can he know why? God is the Earth-Shaker, the Lord of the Pleiades; how can little man contend with Him? He can decide as He wills. He can toss aside human protestations of justice, pleas for pity, claims of right—and who can deny Him the freedom to do so?

It is bold, despairing poetry. Job paints the picture of a God who is an elemental force, a tyrant, beyond man's questioning, a God, in short, to make the weak and heavy-laden lose hope—and yet a God who has sometimes taken shape from the preaching of much later centuries when stress upon God's sovereignty has lost sight of His love, and the everlasting fact that Christ revealed Him.

Job's bitter hopelessness touches on impiety. It is the product of a mind distraught. Verse 23 touches the limit of sharp bitterness. Such a deity has too often haunted the sick imagination of man. Such were the gods of the Epicureans, described well by Tennyson in the *Lotus Eaters*:

> *. . . they lie beside their nectar, and the bolts are hurl'd*
> *Far below them in the valleys, and the clouds are lightly*
> *curl'd*
> *Round their golden houses, girdled with the gleaming world:*
> *Where they smile in secret, looking over wasted lands,*
> *Blight and famine, plague and earthquake, roaring deeps*
> *and fiery sands,*
> *Clanging fights, and flaming towns, and sinking ships, and*
> *praying hands.*
> *But they smile, they find a music centred in a doleful song*
> *Streaming up, a lamentation and an ancient tale of*
> *wrong . . .*

And then, most movingly, the complaints turn more directly into prayer. It is as though the last verses of the chapter (9.33–35) open the thought of a Mediator, and in the light of an unconscious prophecy Job's spirit grows calmer. He still speaks bitterly (10.1–8) but the wild words become more gentle.

A great dramatist of Greece, Aeschylus, the Shakespeare of Athens, once framed such a prayer to Zeus:

> *Zeus, whosoe'er indeed he be,—*
> *In that name, so it please him, hear.*
> *Zeus, for my help is none but he;—*
> *Conjecture through creation free*
> *I cast, and cannot find his peer,*
> *With this strange load upon my mind*
> *So burdening, only Zeus I find*
> *To lift and fling it sheer.*

Catch the accent of man's ancient longing, which Abraham Lincoln put in simpler prose: 'I have been driven many times to my knees by the overwhelming conviction that I had nowhere else to go. My own wisdom, and that of all about me, seemed insufficient for the day.'

74 : Zophar

Job 11; John 8.1-11

Presumably Zophar was the youngest of the three. He has waited properly till now to speak, and, screwing his courage to the point of utterance, has not caught the pathos and the pain of what Job has just said to God. Hence his immoderate and harsh attack. Lies, mockery, words, words, words—when all was plain to Zophar's mind! Job simply did not understand what it meant to be clean in God's eyes. He was wilfully blind to truth.

Consider the self-righteousness of it all. Job must have sinned, or Job would not have lost all that which he had quite manifestly lost! Zophar himself was prosperous, and untouched by such evil. It followed that Zophar had fulfilled all righteousness. Eliphaz has the makings of a prophet. Bildad can claim to be something of a sage, for all the ready-made pattern of his solutions. Zophar is neither saint nor philosopher, but a simple fellow held in the grip of his own dogmatism. Such people are sorry counsellors for those confronting some real problem or some overwhelming trouble. They set forth some simple dogmas which drive the afflicted to despair—'all doubt has some sin as its cause', 'anxiety is lack of faith', 'depression is lack of trust'. Prescribed texts prove it all.

Such people, the Zophars of this world, are extroverts, people without imagination, unsympathetic, not from a cultivated cruelty, but from sheer inability to understand more complicated characters. They are suspicious of all subtlety, their religion is a plain system of punishment and material reward, they have no difficulties, and no perplexities because they are unable to grasp the issues which occasion them. They are invincibly self-righteous, usually of sound constitution and good health, always comfortably situated, not infrequently affluent—and useless in the dark hours of the soul, a peril in the sick room, and a menace in the pulpit. In the mercy of God their naïve faith seems seldom to be drastically tested.

75 : Job's Loneliness

Job 12, 13 and 14

Zophar's hurtful words rouse Job to a sharp reply, ironical (12.2), bitter (13.4 f.). He has been called a fool (11.12). He had held, he knew, an elder's reputation for wisdom, but now he was despised by lesser men who were convinced by his visible misfortune that all his past was sham.

As for Zophar's simple doctrine, let them look around. Out in the desert stood the tents of evil men, the very Bedouin who have looted Job's own goods, whose god was their sword ('who bring their god in their hand', 12.6). What a living refutation of automatic judgement, he seems to say, was the very existence of such unjudged wickedness. Evil *can* prosper, and there is no simple explanation.

There is great mystery. What of nature's self? Drought and flood come mysteriously as the wind, and in the ebb and flux of power in the world of men, no rules of right or wrong, justice or injustice, seem to be discernible. Nor are laws obvious in the vicissitudes of empire and of human right. Neither the Old Testament chroniclers nor the prophets would agree with Job in this, but Job was in a mood of dark disillusionment, and the world was chaos to him. Perhaps this was a reaction too violent to the neat solutions offered by his three friends.

He was disposed to insist that God should make it plain (13.3). Why not? Was it not, he asks (13.4–13), rather they than he who blasphemed God by their smooth and ordered doctrine? God *must* be just, He *must* listen (13.14 f.), perilous though it might be to demand such explanation. Suffering alone gave leave for such presumptuousness. 'Man's body is so small,' said Tagore once, 'his capacity for suffering so very great.'

And his time so brief. Chapter 14 is one of the great

sombre passages of the book. Job had no grasp of immortality. Euripides, son of brilliant Athens, struck a note as sad in the chorus of a play:

> *If any far-off state there be*
> *Dearer to life than mortality,*
> *The hand of death hath hold thereof,*
> *And mists are under and mists above.*
> *The other life is a fountain sealed,*
> *The depths below us are unrevealed,*
> *And we float on legends for ever.*

The hope for which Job did not dare to reach came with Christ and His victory over death, but Job's passion in prayer and poetry was stirred and spurred by the looming victory of the grave.

Questions and themes for study and discussion on Studies 66–75

1. Trouble and God's will.
2. What was 'the lie of Eden'?
3. What is the significance of the home in life's experience?
4. The Christian and despair. Can moods of darkness always be condemned?
5. Slick solutions of life's problems—are they still to be heard?
6. Piety in prayer. The language of prayer.
7. Proof-texts in Christian evangelism—their use and misuse.
8. Why is John 1.18 so important a verse for the understanding of God?
9. What qualities are required in a Christian counsellor for youth, the sick, the mentally ill, the highly intelligent—and other types of people, in your experience?

THE PERSON OF CHRIST

His Return (1)

76 : Before the End

Matthew 24.1–14

The apostolic certainty of the return of Christ was rooted in the teaching of our Lord Himself on this subject. In this great chapter, His teaching on the Last Things emerges from the disciples' twofold question in v. 3 about the destruction of the Temple (2) and His coming. It seems clear that these events were closely associated in their thinking, but our Lord's reply does not imply acceptance of a close temporal connection between them. Two perspectives are in view in His teaching, and this complicates interpretation. Although some of His statements clearly refer to the fall of Jerusalem and others just as clearly to the end of the age, some could apply to either.

In vs. 4–14 Jesus speaks of general matters, principles almost, applying equally to A.D. 70 and to the End. He says in effect: 'These are to be the general characteristics of the age; in greater or lesser degree this is how things will be in the world until I come again.' So many of them reveal the instability of this present order, affected as it is by sin, and reveal the necessity for the coming of God's order, the only really stable one, which is to be ushered in by the return of Christ. He instances in particular three facts: imposters in religion (5, 11), wars and rumours of wars (6 f.), affliction and persecution (9 f.). He exhorts, however, against discouragement (6), for these are the circumstances in which the gospel will be preached in every age. There are no ideal conditions in which to work for Christ; there will always be opposition. But the gospel will be preached (14). This is the one message that can bring the stability of the new order into human life as it is lived in the old world, for, as Paul reminds us, 'if any one is in Christ, he is a new creation; the old has passed away, behold, the new has come' (2 Cor. 5.17). Patient endurance will result in final salvation. Here then our Lord's realistic teaching makes us aware of the fact that, until His return, we live in an evil world, but we do so with a great hope in Christ burning in our hearts.

77 : Tribulation and the Son of Man's Return

Matthew 24.15–28

The great eschatological discourse of our Lord continues. All the troubles and trials of which the earlier verses speak find their climax in the teaching of these verses. A time of great tribulation is described, and this is indicative of the kind of conditions to be expected throughout the course of the age. Everything here is applicable to A.D. 70, and took place then. Although this is true, some of the language at least suggests a further and deeper fulfilment at the approaching end-time. In our study of Isa. 7.1–17 (Study No. 21), we saw another example of the principle of double fulfilment. The emphasis on tribulation in v. 21 indicates that in this time of crisis the pressure (for that is the literal meaning of the word translated 'tribulation' there) that is a constant factor in every age will be greatly intensified.

Something more then than the fall of Jerusalem is in view, viz. nothing less than the great climax of evil prior to Christ's coming. This means that what might otherwise have filled the hearts of God's people with fear itself contains a message of hope, for beyond the tribulation lies the coming. The application to more than one event is confirmed by the reference to Daniel (15), for this prophecy was certainly fulfilled in 168 B.C. when Antiochus Epiphanes, the Seleucid ruler of Syria who claimed authority over the Jews in Palestine, erected an image of Zeus in the Temple. Christ's use of the language of Daniel to describe something yet to happen

109

gives it a multiple meaning, for if it had a more immediate fulfilment in 168 B.C., and a later one in A.D 70, why should it be thought unlikely that yet another fulfilment should lie in the future, at the end? This means that every onslaught of persecution, every time of trial and difficulty for the Church, has been used by her Lord to make her ask, 'Is He coming soon?'. Such experiences, difficult as they may be, are good for us if they make us live not only in the light of the Christ who has come, but of that same Christ's return.

78 : The Signs of His Coming

Matthew 24.29–44

This next section of the Olivet prophecy certainly looks beyond the fall of Jerusalem to the coming of Christ. Three points specially should be noted. First (29–31), the terms describing Christ's coming—clouds of heaven, power and great glory, the trumpet call, the gathering of the elect—correspond to 1 Cor. 15.51 ff.; 1 Thess. 4.15 ff.; Rev. 10.7, and consistency of interpretation demands that we take all these passages as referring to the same things. Comparing Scripture with Scripture is necessary if we are to avoid anarchy of interpretation. The reference to cosmic disturbances associated with the end-time (29) bears witness to the biblical teaching that the sin of man affects the whole creation, and this explains our Lord's language here. In the last days when evil rises to the summit of its arrogance in its defiance of God, the very universe will reel under the impact of the clash.

Secondly, the parable of the fig tree (32–35) may be taken as an ordinary metaphor, meaning that as it is certain that summer will follow when the first leaves are seen on the fig tree, so also the coming of Christ will follow these signs (29). But there may be a deeper meaning, although interpreters are not all agreed on the matter. The fig tree was a symbol of Israel, God's chosen people. Perhaps Jesus is indicating that the Jews are God's signpost in history, and that when things happen with the Jews it is a sign that God is going to act.

In this connection, 'generation' (34) can have the meaning of 'a race or family of people'. It is not without significance that the Jewish people, in spite of repeated attempts to destroy them, have remained in existence because God wills them to do so.

Thirdly, Christ ends with a solemn exhortation in which the attitudes of carelessness and watchfulness are contrasted. The unthinking complacency, indifference and ignorance that characterized the days of Noah (37–39) will be repeated at the end-time. It is a picture of the secularization of society. Over against this, He stresses the necessity of watchfulness in view of the sudden and unannounced nature of His coming (42–44). Here we find the true purpose of prophecy: its challenge is not speculative, but moral. We do not understand it aright unless it makes us watch and pray.

79 : Reckoning Time

Matthew 25.31–46

This picture of the final judgement bases judgement fairly and squarely on works, while faith is not mentioned. This is perplexing and disturbing to many, but there is no suggestion that salvation can be earned by good works; rather faith is presupposed. A true believer is 'created in Christ Jesus for good works' (Eph. 2.10), and where these are lacking, a question mark must be placed over against a man's profession. Good works do not themselves argue that a man is justified before God, but their absence shows he is not. 'Faith without works is dead', 'Faith working through love' —these are the propositions Jesus deals with here. That this is how to interpret the passage is corroborated by the words in v. 34, 'Come, O blessed of my Father, inherit . . .' One does not earn or deserve an inheritance: it is a gift, and comes through standing in a certain relationship to the one who bestows it. Above all, those who do inherit are said to be blessed by the Father. This is how salvation begins, and this fact forbids us to reverse Jesus' words and deduce the possession of salvation from the evidence of good works.

For this would mean that every humanitarian or philanthropic work would argue a Christian testimony, which is far from being the same. Giving a cup of cold water is a kindly act, but it may or may not be a Christian one. It is only Christian if it is done by a Christian.

It is sins of omission, not of commission, that Jesus condemns here. Men are blind and impervious to human need because they are preoccupied with themselves. The reason why we fail to feed the hungry and visit the sick is that so many other things occupy our attention. This is why the primary need is to be blessed by the Father, for the blessing He gives is a cross that slays the self-life and re-creates us new in Christ for self-forgetful service to others. Judgement, then, is on the basis of love. Acts and attitudes of love are what salvation, when real, always produces. The fruit of the Spirit is love, and love is what Christ will look for on the day of judgement. 'Have you loved?' He will ask. We should beware however of misunderstanding what the New Testament means by 'love'. A Christian's works are produced by Christian love, which is not simply love for man but love for Christ's sake and out of love for *God*.

Questions and themes for study and discussion on Studies 76–79

1. In the light of Jesus' words in Matt. **24**, how true is it to say that every crisis time in history is a foreshadowing of His coming?

2. What are the main differences between the true Christ and false Christs?

3. How are we to relate the 'signs' of the approaching end in Matt. **24**.29 ff. to the emphasis in vs. 36 ff. on the suddenness and unexpectedness of Christ's coming?

4. 'Son of Man', 'King', 'my Father', 'Lord'—what do these expressions tell us about Christ's glory? (read Matt. **25**.31–46 in the light of its opening verse).

CHARACTER STUDIES

80 : Eliphaz Again

Job 15, 16 and 17

In this chapter we see a little more of the weighty and dignified Eliphaz, although he is more on the edge of his temper here. His personality is well maintained in his discourse. 'I have seen . . .' (**15**.17) still records his appeal to his own unique experience. He is mightily suspicious of reasoned argument—the word 'crafty' appears in both of his speeches. He has his set quotations or favourite sayings (**15**.15 repeats **4**.18) and they substitute for discussion.

Eliphaz first expostulates with Job (**15**.1–13), whom in irony he calls 'wise'. He thinks Job guilty of plain profanity, or with an obtuse and quite inadequate consciousness of sin. He bends his efforts now to persuade Job to confess his sin (14–17). Could he but make Job realize the surpassing holiness of God, Job, he is sure, will see sin as he, Eliphaz, sees it, and acknowledge his shortcomings. All that is lacking in the argument is any consciousness of shortcoming on Eliphaz' own part! He is calmly and exasperatingly righteous.

Job's reply shows the futility of all his senior friend has to say. He is weary of their unfeeling arguments, and he reproaches the three of them for their failure to give him any grain of comfort (**16**.1–6). After all, he continues, and seems with the dull, despairing words to descend deeper into bitterness, after all, what can he expect of men when God Himself has set him up as a target (12), a fortress wall to batter down (14), and left him without pity to be a spectacle of grief and desolation. Nor can he see hope. He has 'sewn himself in sackcloth' (15), as though to demonstrate the permanence of his situation. He has faced the ultimate, and come to terms with death, and death's sting is that it is without meaning, flung upon him with contumely by a God who does not care. It is terrible language, this speech of the soul's midnight. Job, like those of his day, saw no clear hope beyond death, and so it became of agonizing, desperate importance that he should be vindicated before the horror of last dissolution laid hold of him. And now all hope of this seemed vain.

81 : Job's Faith

Job 18 and 19

The art of the writer of this book is tremendous. He makes his hard and mistaken characters say the most outrageous things plausibly and effectively. Bildad, the narrow-minded exponent of traditional reason, is on the attack again. With cruel and unfeeling rigour, and in a tone of bitterness, Bildad attacks Job once more. He simply cannot understand how anyone can reject the established findings of ancient wisdom. The case of Job must necessarily have its explanation. It must be according to simple ancient rules. Job is wilfully misunderstanding the situation. He is being punished for sin, and he is adding to the sin by denying the patent fact. Eliphaz, of course, said as much, but Eliphaz had the attitude of a cultured man. Bildad is a crude and simple soul, a hopeless failure in any situation of stress. He knows all the rules! And stress is obvious, deepening and deadly. Job speaks of the utter rejection in which he finds himself. Wife, children, friends, have alike cast him aside. Then comes one of the most remarkable passages in the book. Job has to this point betrayed no hope of vindication in another life, of which he has no clear knowledge, but now, in a gush of faith, some conception of a life beyond the grave emerges. It can hardly be interpreted in any other way. Ellison gives a bold translation of 19.25–27, which is a fair rendering. Translation must not, as it too often is, be determined by pre-conceived theology, and fixed opinions of what the writer knew, and did not know. In Psa. **22** and Isa. **53** the sufferer on a surge of passionate perception is enabled to pierce through to new truth, and that is what Job does here: 'I know that my Vindicator lives and will yet stand upon the earth; and after my skin has been thus destroyed, then without my flesh I shall see God, whom I shall see on my side, and my eyes shall see to be un-estranged.' Then, nearly overwhelmed by what has formed on his lips, Job ends: 'My heart fails with longing within me.' Job's darkest hour has become his finest.

82 : Job Exaggerates

Job 20 and 21

Job's closing words, which appeared to counter-attack and threaten his hard friends with judgement, infuriate Zophar. In some indignation he paints a portrait of the wicked man to match Eliphaz' effort in ch. **15**. The only notable lines added are his insistence on the brevity of the evil person's enjoyment of the pleasures of sin. He is obviously in some difficulty over the lack of real and specific charges to level against Job, so he makes a thrust in the dark. The exploitation of the peasantry was a common sin among the rich in the old world of these events, so he boldly suggests that Job has heartlessly downtrodden the poor. He has done it slyly, but God has seen and punished. Job attacks boldly in his reply. Zophar has too rashly alleged that the evil man soon perishes. In fact, he says, this is demonstrably not the case. Job un-doubtedly exaggerates. Perhaps this is for an unexpected reason. At his greatest point of tension and of faith, he has, as we have seen, broken through to a conception of divine justice and judgement which takes into account a vindication and a reckoning beyond this life. He will, he knows, in a sudden burst of confidence, be shown ultimate and perfect justice. Does it not equally follow that evil can only meet its final retribution in another dimension of being? Zophar has claimed that all happens according to a fixed and immutable law. The doer suffers. Sin reaps its own reward and always reaps its own reward.

Job knows that this is not so, and, in the stress of debate, he over-corrects. He sets against his opponent's too simple picture of majestic and automatic retribution, a rather shocking picture of sin's immunity. Measuring merely by the yardstick of superficial retribution, and leaving out of account the wealth of the mind and heart that evil is denied, it is obvious to any observer that the sinners of this world often get what they seek and die in their beds, old in evil, as frequently, perhaps, as they meet with visible judgement. Judgement is many-sided, and not always to be seen. But observe the humanity of it all. Zophar was part right, part wrong. Job, in reply, shares his error. But he is now more quiet, more collected. He has his vision.

83 : Job's Desolation

Job 22, 23 and 24

Eliphaz, best of Job's friends though he is, returns to the attack under the power of his dominant obsession—that truth which had come to him in the strange vision of the night. He will not have this firm rock in any way questioned. It makes him wildly angry when anyone seems to question in any way the validity of what had happened to him, the experience which had become his boast. Quite cruelly, he picks up what Job himself says of wicked men and deliberately aims it back at him (21.14, f.; 22.12–17). And having said his harsh say, hardly realizing its hardness, Eliphaz returns to his appeal.

Faced with such crass misunderstanding, Job touches the depths of despair again. Job's longing for a way to God (23.3) forms one of the most poignant verses in Scripture. It is life's most terrible experience to feel that God is remote, withdrawn and difficult to find, removed from comprehension, approach, hearing.

116

Gladly I'd march though the way were drear,
If I could but see the oasis near,
Or out in the wilderness only hear
Crying the Voice of One ...

Job could see nothing but the mirage, hear no sound of comfort in his howling wilderness. He felt alone, abandoned, helpless. Perhaps the awesome cry of desolation on the Cross (Matt. 27.46) shows that Christ in His humanity plumbed these depths, and tasted this bitter cup. Nor, as Job contends, is it always the tyranny which brings such pain. Hope deferred, stress of mind, the bitterness of loss, even prayer inexplicably unanswered, can bring such testing. God, in His wisdom, but always for the sufferer's ultimate blessing, sometimes allows the Adversary to have his way. The Christian has so much more than Job had to make such Gethsemanes more plain. Christ trod this path, right to the Cross, and the Cross became the most creative event in the history of man. Christ for ever shows that pain has meaning. But what a picture is Job who knew not where he might find Him! We know. John 1.18 is the secret, and in Christ we can always find Almighty God. Read Heb. 10.19–22 in Phillips or the NEB.

84 : Job Stands Fast

Job 28, 29 and 30

Job is still passionately groping for God, and in a burst of poetry he pictures questing man probing the depths of earth to wrest its treasures of precious metal, seeking, discovering with toil and effort—but not finding God. Some of the more modern versions make his description of ancient mining more vivid, the digging, driving of deep shafts, the crushing of the ore. In a passage which reads like Prov. 8, Job tells where true wisdom is to be found, culminating in the fine words of 28.28. Job has laid hold of supreme truth; that life's problems begin to find solution only when God is set first, made supreme, and trusted.

In the next chapter the mood changes. In the midst of

117

affliction and distress the memory of past happiness is a sharp and painful memory. In a surge of new misery, Job remembers the peace and plenty which once were his when he lay in the light of God's love. Keenest of his regrets is the memory of the esteem and good will in which men held him. In beautiful words he tells how he had, in times past, used his wealth as a good man would use it in a world of poverty, to lift the burden of the heavy-laden, to uphold justice, and sweeten the community in which he lived.

It is a beautiful chapter, this bright flashback to the days of rest and joy. But, such is the manner of man, that those whom he had helped, and those who had paid him the rightful measure of reverence and regard, now turned to dishonour him in the contemptible manner of men. Ingratitude is hard to bear, and naturally enough, for, as Jonathan Swift once said, that noisome vice 'sums up all the evil of man'. And perhaps the best known quotation from Shakespeare is on the same theme—and touches Job's sombre mood:

> Blow, blow, thou winter wind,
>   thou art not so unkind
> as man's ingratitude . . .
>   Freeze, freeze, thou bitter sky,
> thou dost not bite so nigh
>   as benefits forgot.

It is a sad picture with which we leave Job—an ageing man who expected to die in peace and who cannot understand his catastrophe. God's word to him is outside our theme. We have sought a man—and how human!

85 : Elihu

Job 32 and 33

All this time a young man has been listening, deferential before his elders. The three older men, and Job himself, have fallen silent. There is no more to say. The discourses have, however, left Elihu angry. He worships a greater God than they, and the discovery of the fact infuriates him. Elihu had expected understanding, instruction, final wisdom, from men so much more experienced than himself, and now he realizes that it is not the lapse of years or the accumulation of experience which makes for wisdom. God instructs, God makes wise, God enlightens, and it therefore follows that a young man has something worth while to say if he has the inspiration of God's Spirit.

It is excellent characterization. Elihu has an assurance, and a certainty of rectitude which jars a little; but who, remembering youth, and the stark simplicities of first conviction, cannot see a dash of self in the portrait? It is also worth observing that God rebukes the others, as the book moves to its climax, but spares Elihu actual rebuke—He merely dismisses his counsel as inconclusive. Youth has a right to speak. Youth can proclaim truth. Youth can be enlightened by God. 'Let no man despise your youth,' said Paul to Timothy. Moreover young Elihu has meticulously observed the proprieties. He has not rushed in, nor said a word until the rest ended in frustration.

His whole speech should be read. It is eloquent and cogent. Elihu, unlike the older men with their prefabricated solutions, does not accuse Job of gross misdemeanour. Nevertheless, having laid down his premise of God's surpassing holiness, he cannot but maintain that the whole explanation of the problem must somewhere lie in the guilt, the fault, of the afflicted. He suggests that this fault is spiritual pride, a conclusion prompted by Job's survey of his standing and acceptance in his happier years. Indeed, does not the reading of that eloquent and moving passage suggest a certain naïve satisfaction on Job's part against which there may be put a tiny question mark? All of us can echo every word. This is how we all think in times of stress when we look back on days of tranquillity. But most of us refrain from exposing pain so frankly to the ever-present Elihu. Elihu saw the opening and shot his bolt through this innocent joint in the armour. Alas, as the old Moody hymn has it, in this world, ungrateful, insensitive, we must often 'go, bury our sorrow'.

Questions and themes for study and discussion on Studies 80–85

1. On what is the Christian belief in another life most securely based?
2. What has the New Testament to say about a vindicator?
3. What are the essential qualities of a comforter?
4. Is justice done in this life, ever? never? sometimes? visibly? invisibly?
5. Compare Job's experience with Elijah's.
6. Can a fundamentally ungrateful person be a Christian?

THE PERSON OF CHRIST

His Return (2)

86 : 'Sincere and without Offence'

Philippians 1.1–11; 3.17–4.1

Paul speaks here of the return of Christ in relation to the completion of the work of grace in the believer. In giving thanks for the Philippians, he expresses his confidence that the good work of redemption that has been begun in them would continue without remission until the coming of Christ consummated it. The recurring reference to the day of Christ (1.6, 10) shows that Paul's eyes were always upon the return of Christ and that he would have his readers to live also in the light of that great event.

Two things are said about this 'good work'. First, there is a marvellously mysterious interaction of divine sovereignty and human responsibility involved in it, not merely in the sense expressed in the famous words of 2.12 f., but in the sense that Paul himself had responsibility in the matter. 'The ground of my confidence that this good work will continue,' he says, 'is that I hold you in my heart'—i.e. within the divine sovereignty at work in salvation and sanctification there is a place for the prayers of God's people, for He uses it to begin and continue the work of grace in men's souls. The kind of prayer He uses is indicated in vs. 9–11; its true spirit in v. 8, and its fruits in vs. 10 f.

Secondly, in 3.17 ff. the prospect of the day of Christ which will consummate the good works of God is held out as an incentive to holy and steadfast living. The coming Christ is our Saviour. At the cross He secured our salvation. Now He is glorified and not only will our bodies be made like His but this will be done by that almighty power which He wields as the risen Lord and which will secure the complete fulfilment of all the purposes of God through Him. Paul encourages the Philippians to live as he and those who have followed his example live—as citizens of Christ's heavenly kingdom. A day will come when their lowly bodies —marred by sin, yet bearing even now the marks of restoration to the divine image through His good work in them— will be changed and will share to the full the nature and inherent qualities of His glorified body. This is incentive enough to walk the way of the cross (**3**.7–14), following the apostolic example.

87 : The Comfort of His Coming

1 Thessalonians 4.13–18

Paul wrote these words to correct the Thessalonians' misunderstanding of what he had taught them about the return of Christ during his ministry at Thessalonica. While they awaited His coming some of their number had died, and the question that now worried them was: had they been robbed by death of the Christian hope? Had it passed for ever beyond their grasp because they had died before Christ came to take His people to Himself? Paul's answer is that there will be no difference between those who are alive at Christ's coming and those who have already died, for the coming of Christ will usher in the resurrection of the dead, and those alive will be caught up with them to meet the Lord in the air. There is no cause, then, to sorrow over those now asleep in Him.

Christ's coming is a personal return. There have been attempts to spiritualize it to mean either the coming of the Spirit at Pentecost or the coming of death to the believer. The personal character of His return is taught too plainly and too frequently for such attempts to gain any real plausibility. We should compare these verses with 1 Cor. **15**.51 f.; Matt. **24**.29-31 and Rev. **10**.7 to see that Paul is speaking of the last trumpet at the end of time, which heralds the judgement and the day of God. This necessarily means that the resurrection of believers is part of the general resurrection referred to in John **5**.28 f. and Acts **24**.15 (cf. also Matt. **13**.30, 41 f. 49; Rom. **2**.5–10).

A passage like this makes us realize the central importance of our Lord's return for the whole New Testament presentation of the future and fulfilment of the purposes of God. Resurrection and consummation both await His coming, and what lies beyond this is still presented in terms of Christ. 'So shall we always be with the Lord.'

88 : 'Like a Thief in the Night'

1 Thessalonians 5.1–11

The opening verses of ch. **5** continue the emphasis of the closing part of ch. **4**—the return of Christ. There, however, Paul had dealt with the Thessalonians' ignorance and with problems arising from misunderstanding, while here he reminds them of the implications of things they know very well (2). To know, as they did, about the conditions which would precede the coming of Christ, and, above all, about its unexpectedness and suddenness, bringing terror to the unprepared, ought to produce in them the fruits of watchfulness (4), sobriety (6) and hope (8). The illustration of the thief is a link with our Lord's own teaching (Matt. **24**.43).

Paul stresses here the absolute contrast between light and darkness, day and night (4 ff.). No sentimentalism should make us blunt the sharp edge of these distinctions. Ultimately there are only two possibilities for men: they belong to Christ or to the devil. Indeed, one of the effects of the day of the Lord will be to expose and confirm such distinctions for ever. Our Lord spoke of Himself as the Light of the World, and it is our attitude to Him which determines whether we are sons of the light or the darkness (John **8**.12).

The apostle refers to those who are not Christ's as asleep (6 f.). The unbeliever sometimes suggests that the Christian lives in an unreal world of fantasy. The very reverse is the case. Christ is the Truth and those alone who know Him are awake to things as they are. Reality comes through waking out of sleep, whether in time or in eternity.

Although ch. **5** may give the impression of dealing with the subject more in terms of an event ('that day') than of a Person, vs. 9 f. make it quite clear (as does 4.13–18, which is continuous with it) that this is not really so. The 'day' is important because it is *His* day.

89 : Judgement and Vindication

2 Thessalonians 1

2 Thessalonians was written to correct misunderstanding and misinterpretation of 1 Thessalonians. The main theme is the same in both, viz. the return of Christ. This is dealt with here in two different aspects, showing the end result of a well defined and distinct process at work in two classes of men, the unbelieving and the believing.

First, the coming of Christ will mean a judgement of retribution on the ungodly, who are introduced here as the source of the Thessalonians' persecutions and afflictions (4). The fact that the Thessalonians are standing firm argues the unseen presence of the Lord upholding them, and this means two things: He uses the tribulation to bring their faith to perfection; and such a situation, in which evil men oppress the good, calls aloud for judgement, and proclaims its certainty. The universe is built on moral lines, and God must vindicate the righteous and punish the wicked, hence this twofold manifestation of judgement, in which rest comes to God's people and affliction to the evildoers (6 f.). Nor is this arbitrary, but the fruition of a continuing attitude of unbelief. Paul distinguishes between those who 'do not know God' and those who 'do not obey the gospel' (8), i.e. the Gentiles and the Jews (cf. Rom. 1.18–2.1 ff.). The Jews have had the divine revelation, first in the law and later in the preaching of the gospel; therefore they are without excuse. But the Gentiles' ignorance is also culpable, for they refused the light of nature and of conscience that might have led them into the knowledge of God.

Secondly, the 'bright side' of judgement is Christ's coming to be glorified in His saints (10), the final consummation for those who, called of God (11) through the preaching of the gospel (10b), have responded to His word, enabling Him to fulfil all His perfect will in them (11). This is described in both negative and positive terms—rest from affliction (7), and glorification (10, 12). The coming of the all-glorious Christ will be the power that transfigures us, because 'the inner glory of faith will be drawn out to its object, and not only shine forth, but in doing so transform the mortal into the immortal. And the beauty of the glorified saint will be seen to be of the same essential beauty as that of the glorified Saviour' (W. Still).

90 : Christ and Antichrist

2 Thessalonians 2.1–12

The Thessalonians had apparently been disturbed by teaching which claimed that the day of the Lord had already come (2), and Paul writes to safeguard against deception (3 ff.). He points out first that, as he had previously taught them (5), Christ's coming must necessarily be preceded by 'the rebellion' and the appearance of the man of lawlessness (3). What this rebellion is he does not specify, but the context indicates a final, climactic revolt against God headed up in an individual who is the incarnation of evil, the Antichrist. There have been many antichrists in history (1 John 2.18), but Paul has in mind the final manifestation in the last days, and until then Christ will not come again. The Antichrist's coming into the open is, however, the work of God, who thus draws him out in order finally to destroy him. Verse 8 shows us how utterly the Lord Jesus will demonstrate by this act of judgement His supremacy and His power over the Antichrist.

Next, in vs. 6 f., Paul refers to a restraining power at work preventing the full expression of evil. He does not explain what he means, and we are left to speculate. Widely different interpretations have been suggested, such as the Holy Spirit, or the Roman Empire, or some angelic being. It is best to see a reference to the principle of law and order, which Paul envisages as being overthrown in the last time, allowing evil to erupt with frightful consequences for the world.

Thirdly, Paul describes something of these frightful consequences (9–12). The activities of this fiendish incarnation of evil are horrific in their implications. Note the blasphemous counterfeit that Satan's work represents here: the man of sin 'comes' as Christ has His coming; he works by supernatural power, as Christ worked by the power of God; he works miracles as Christ did. This is very alarming, and but for one consideration might lead to despair: those who are deceived and perish do so because they have refused to love the truth. Men are not subject to blind forces of fate; moral issues control human destinies, and it is a wrong attitude to the truth that ultimately leads to total deception, and want of sympathy with it that finally damns them. This is no arbitrary vengeance on God's part (cf. Rom. 1.24–28): He is left with no other option than to leave men to the consequences of their own final choice (11). He does so with tears in His eyes (cf. Luke 19.41–44).

91 : The Lamb's Great Bridal Feast

Revelation 19.6–16

The vision John unfolds here is of the final consummation of history and the victory of Christ. It consists of two images; that of the marriage of the Lamb (7 ff.), and that of the victory of the Warrior-King (11 ff.). The choral praise in vs. 6 ff. answers the voice from the throne in v. 5, and describes the jubilation of heaven at the triumph of righteousness. But the preoccupation is not so much with the overthrow of evil as with the glorious reality of the marriage of the Lamb to His Bride. The imagery of Eastern marriage, with the interval between betrothal and marriage during which the bride prepared herself, is fruitful in spiritual illustration. The fine linen (8) with which she is clothed corresponds to the work of sanctification in the lives of God's people: how they are attired on the marriage day will depend on how they live in the interval between their betrothal to Christ and His coming for them. Suffering for His sake, and the sanctifying effect this has on spiritual life, will enlarge their capacity for grandeur and glory in the world to come, just as a wife who brings to her marriage a sound training in practical godliness and faithful living will immeasurably enrich her married life. Furthermore, marriage is not only an end but a beginning also; it is the end of the longing and the waiting, but it is not the end of the story. It opens out into a richer and fuller experience, with unimagined joys and delights, enchantments, responsibilities and privileges.

This glorious consummation is brought about by Christ's coming in power to judge the world (11 ff.). The portrayal of the Faithful and True, The Word of God, King of kings and Lord of lords, almost beggars description. To see the King in His beauty, to see Him come thus, the joy of the universe—joy to those who have owned Him Lord, terror to those who have refused His gospel—this is ultimate reality, for weal or woe. The only thing that will matter then will be to have been on His side, and to have His smile of recognition and commendation. Even to read of it is benediction enough, but to participate in this great event and experience it, defies description. 'Lo, this is our God; we have waited for Him' (Isa. 25.9).

92 : The Urgency of the Gospel Appeal

Revelation 22.6–21

In this epilogue John insists on the authenticity of the visions (6, 18, 19). They are not a series of predictions by a far-sighted man, but a revelation given from above, an unveiling of the truth about our world and of the certainties of things to come.

The solemn urgency of vs. 10–17 reminds us that the purpose of the prophecy is not speculative, or merely to give a better knowledge of the principles that govern the world, but that we should be challenged to come to grips with the truth of the gospel. It is eternal destinies that are at stake, and how men react here to Christ and His gospel will determine their destiny. Hence the warning in v. 10: at all costs men must hear the message and be given opportunity to respond to it before it is too late (12). This is the force of v. 11, 'Let the evildoer still do evil . . .' What a man becomes in this life he will remain for ever; inevitably, inexorably, by their reaction to the gospel, men are deciding their destiny now. Acts, habits, attitudes—these are the fateful choices by which men determine character and its outcome in the eternal order. By nature we all make the wrong choice and invite against ourselves the law by which act ripens into habit, habit into character and character into destiny. But God is greater than this inevitable process of hardening; He is Alpha and Omega, i.e. sin does not have the last word. He can break into the terrible chain of cause and effect that drags men down, and in Christ invites them to come to One who breaks the power of sin and cleanses from all its defilement (14).

Hence the blessedly sweet invitation in v. 17 to 'Come', given by the Spirit and the Bride. The tugging at the heart, the stirring within us, the sudden awareness of the persuasiveness and power of the message—all this is the Spirit saying 'Come.' The Church adds her persuasion to the Spirit's pleading, praying men on Christ's behalf to be reconciled to God (2 Cor. 5.20).

Finally, the warning against adding to or subtracting from the words of the prophecy (18 f.) is crowned by our Lord's testimony to the imminence of His coming and the Church's glad and eager cry, 'Amen. Come, Lord Jesus!'

Questions and themes for study and discussion on Studies 86–92

1. What is the relation between 'pure and blameless' in Phil. 1.10 and 'like his glorious body' in Phil. 3.21?

2. What have Paul's words in 1 Thess. 4.13 ff. to tell us about the nature and significance of Christ's coming?

3. What points of similarity between Paul's teaching in 2 Thess. 1 and that in 1 Thess. 4.13—5.11 make it clear that he is referring to the same event in both passages?

4. What points of comparison are there between Paul's words in 2 Thess. 2 and our Lord's in Matt. 24?

5. What is the relationship of the two images of the consummation of history John uses in Rev. 19 to others used elsewhere, e.g. 'the holy city Jerusalem' in Rev. 21.10 ff.?

6. In setting the appeal of the gospel in the context of the return of Christ, what does Rev. 22. 6–21 tell us about evangelism?